Dedication

To my wife, Peggy Louise.
Thanks for the many years of love and strong support.

About the Author

Robert G. Hoehn has taught earth science, physical science, and biology in the Roseville Joint Union High School District of California since 1963. He has received seven National Summer Science grants from the National Science Foundation and has given numerous presentations to teachers and administrators attending local and state science conventions, workshops, and seminars. He has also served as a mentor teacher in his district.

Mr. Hoehn has a B.A. from San Jose State University and an administration credential from California State University, Sacramento. He is a member of the National Education Association, California Teacher's Association, and California Science Teacher's Association. Author of *Earth Science Curriculum Activities Kit*, 1991, and *Science Starters!*, 1993, both by The Center for Applied Research in Education, he has also published a number of nonfiction books and copymaster sets and over 70 magazine articles on science education, coaching, and baseball/softball strategy.

About This Book

Science Puzzlers! provides a fresh collection of puzzler activities designed to challenge students in upper elementary and middle grades.

The three science areas—life science, physical science, and earth science—offer 150 puzzler activities ranging from basic vocabulary wordsearches to filling-in the terms and mini-problem solvers for creative thinkers.

Each science area is broken down into ten units, five activities for each unit. There are 50 puzzlers per section for a total of 150 activities.

The book benefits students in four ways. They are:

- The variety of activities helps keep student interest high.

- The vocabulary building activities are non-threatening, yet challenging enough to encourage students to strengthen their knowledge of science.

- An occasional riddle or mini-problem sneaks into an activity. The creative thinker with a sense of humor can stimulate the cerebral neurons crying for a challenge.

- Most of the activities can be completed in one class period.

The book serves you, the educator, in four ways. They are:

- You may select up to five activities for each science topic. For example, Section One (Life Science): *The Cell* unit is broken down as follows:
  - All About Cells—A 15-item fill-in activity
  - Structures of the Plant Cell—A 12-term crossword puzzler
  - Rhyming Cell Terms—A 20-rhyming-term puzzler
  - Two Clues—A 15-term fill-in activity
  - Putting It All Together—A 12-term search puzzler

The large variety of activities allows you to select those assignments that fit your specific classroom needs.

- You have 150 activities at your disposal. You may use them as regular classwork, supplemental activities during class, for outside assignments, and for extra-credit projects.

- Each activity can be easily reproduced and made available to every student.

- A Teacher's Answer Key can be found at the end of the book.

Science Puzzlers! will supply you with a diversity of activities to promote thinking and stimulate learning. Select the ones you feel meet your needs and have the best chance of motivating your students.

Robert G. Hoehn
Oakmont High School
Roseville, CA

TABLE OF CONTENTS

Health and Human Diseases

Ecology

PHYSICAL SCIENCE

Energy

Sound

Light

Electricity/Magnetism

EARTH SCIENCE

Minerals

Rocks

Weathering and Erosion

Earth Features

Fossils

Meteorology

Oceanography

Nonrenewable Energy Sources

Renewable Energy Sources

Astronomy

ANSWER KEY
217

SECTION ONE

Life Science

Name _____ Date _____

1. All About Cells

There are 15 cell structures or cellular processes described in the puzzle. If you identify these items, you will reveal the answer to the mystery question.

1. Contains chlorophyll

2. Plays a role in cellular division

3. Outer covering of animal cell

4. Living cellular materials

5. A nucleic acid

6. Cell structure inside the nucleus

7. The powerhouse of the cell

8. Makes up the cell wall

9. Tiny organs within a cell

10. Protein-making site of the cell

11. Stores food, water, etc.

12. All living material surrounding the nucleus

13. Threadlike coils of chromosomes

14. Process by which materials enter and leave a cell through the cell membrane

15. Produced during aerobic respiration

Mystery Question: What material "reads" the genetic information carried by DNA and guides the

protein-making process? _____

2. Structures of the Plant Cell

Across

1. Basic unit of life.
4. The shape of a plant cell.
6. Control center of cellular activity.
8. Green pigment.
9. Inside cellular material that carry out life processes.
11. A cell organelle in which protein is made.
12. Storage areas.

Down

1. Outside protective wall.
2. Endoplasmic _ _ _ _ _ _ _ _ _
3. Energy-producing organelle.
5. Structures containing chlorophyll.
7. A chemical reaction used to produce food.
10. Color of chloroplasts.

3. Rhyming Cell Terms

Find terms related to cells or cellular structures that rhyme with the <u>underlined</u> words. Write the sound-alike terms in the spaces to the right.

1. Rhymes with <u>swell</u>   _____

2. Rhymes with <u>strife</u>   _____

3. Rhymes with <u>propane</u>   _____

4. Rhymes with <u>spasm</u>   _____

5. Rhymes with <u>oriole</u>   _____

6. Rhymes with <u>issue</u>   _____

7. Rhymes with <u>flour mill</u>   _____

8. Rhymes with <u>illusion</u>   _____

9. Rhymes with <u>psychosis</u>   _____

10. Rhymes with <u>vision</u>   _____

11. Rhymes with <u>halitosis</u>   _____

12. Rhymes with <u>school</u>   _____

13. Rhymes with <u>blast</u>   _____

14. Rhymes with <u>high</u>   _____

15. Rhymes with <u>tell</u>   _____

16. Rhymes with <u>psychology</u>   _____

17. Rhymes with <u>crook</u>   _____

18. Rhymes with <u>perspiration</u>   _____

19. Rhymes with <u>tell all</u>   _____ _____ (two words)

20. Rhymes with <u>scene</u>   _____

Name _____ Date _____

4. Two Clues

Use the two clues in the left column to help you identify the terms associated with the plant or animal cell or both. Write the term for each set of clues on the dotted lines to the right of the clues. Unscramble the circled letters in the terms to answer the bonus question.

Two Clues

Term

1. organelle, largest

1. _ _ _ _ _ _ _

2. membrane, water

2. _ _ _ _ _ _ _ _

3. "powerhouses," energy

3. _ _ _ _ ○ _ _ _ _ _ _

4. protein synthesis

4. _ _ _

5. cell wall

5. _ _ _ _ _   ○ _ _ _ (2 words)

6. nucleus, threads

6. _ _ _ _ _ _ _ _ ○

7. sac, storage

7. _ _ _ _ _ _ _

8. division, chromosomes

8. _ ○ _ _ _ _ _

9. acid, genetic

9. _ _ _

10. nucleus, inside

10. _ _ _ ○ _ _ _ _ _

11. movement, molecules

11. _ _ _ ○ _ _ _

12. green, chlorophyll

12. _ _ _ _ _ _ _ _ _ _ _

13. boundary, cellulose

13. _ _ _ _   _ _ _ _ (2 words)

14. round, digestion

14. _ _ _ _ _ _ ○ _

15. living materials

15. _ _ _ _ _ _ _ _ _ _

Bonus Question:

What is the name of the acids found in the nucleus of a cell?

Answer: _____

Name _____ Date _____

5. Putting It All Together

Unscramble the letters of *six* structures scattered inside the plant and animal cell. Write the scrambled terms in the spaces below each diagram. You *must* use *every* letter in *each* cell.

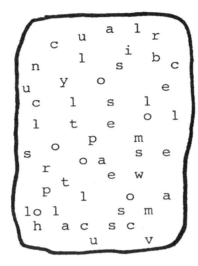

Plant Cell

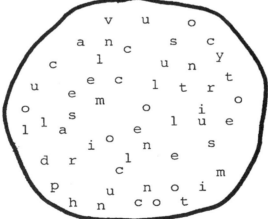

Animal Cell

_____   _____

_____   _____

_____   _____

6. Twenty of Thirty

There are 30 terms related to genetics scattered around the puzzle. Find and circle 20 of the terms in the puzzle. Terms may be up, down, forward, backward and diagonal.

```
m  i  t  o  s  i  s  d  e  e  r  b  n  i
h  y  b  r  i  d  e  a  i  q  g  o  g  a
a  o  t  p  e  t  o  g  y  z  e  e  r  l
g  n  i  r  p  s  f  f  o  p  n  k  e  b
c  h  r  o  m  o  s  o  m  e  e  l  c  i
d  o  r  g  a  n  i  s  m  a  r  t  e  n
e  b  n  a  p  o  c  j  s  p  a  n  s  o
l  m  e  u  n  i  p  s  i  l  t  a  s  p
e  c  r  i  t  s  o  k  w  a  i  n  i  o
l  e  b  e  g  r  v  f  e  n  o  i  v  r
l  l  n  h  c  m  a  c  u  t  n  m  e  g
a  e  p  r  o  t  e  i  n  s  e  o  s  a
g  r  s  n  o  i  t  a  t  u  m  d  i  n
```

<table>
<tr><td>1. hybrid</td><td>11. cross</td><td>21. meiosis</td></tr>
<tr><td>2. gene</td><td>12. generation</td><td>22. albino</td></tr>
<tr><td>3. dna</td><td>13. allele</td><td>23. hemophilia</td></tr>
<tr><td>4. chromosome</td><td>14. offspring</td><td>24. replication</td></tr>
<tr><td>5. genetics</td><td>15. organism</td><td>25. mitosis</td></tr>
<tr><td>6. heredity</td><td>16. probability</td><td>26. pure</td></tr>
<tr><td>7. trait</td><td>17. zygote</td><td>27. inbreed</td></tr>
<tr><td>8. mutation</td><td>18. genotype</td><td>28. recombinant</td></tr>
<tr><td>9. recessive</td><td>19. phenotype</td><td>29. hybridization</td></tr>
<tr><td>10. dominant</td><td>20. protein</td><td>30. pea plants</td></tr>
</table>

On the back of the page, alphabetize the 20 circled terms. Also, describe these terms in no more than *two* words: albino, hemophilia, heredity, zygote, gene, offspring, and mitosis.

7. Missing Letters

Fill in the missing letters for each term in the spaces provided. Then shade in the missing letters in the puzzle. Unscramble the *unshaded* letters to reveal the answer to the mystery question.

1. __ e r __ d i __ y

2. d o __ i n __ __ t

3. __ e c __ s s __ v __

4. t __ a __ t

5. c h __ __ c e

6. i n __ e r __ t

7. p __ __ b a __ i l i t y

8. __ r o __ s

9. r __ t i __

10. h __ b r __ d

h	b	t	a	e
e	h	g	i	a
r	o	s	a	o
s	i	n	r	e
n	y	e	i	n
r	c	m	e	i

Let's see how many questions you can answer by using the letters in the puzzle. You may use a letter more than once.

1. What is the study of heredity called? _____

2. What are the characteristics of an individual called? _____

3. What is the name for structures located on the chromosomes that determine hereditary

   traits? _____

4. What is the term for a new reproductive cell? _____

5. What is a random, unpredictable event in genetics? _____

Mystery Question: What do you call the units of hereditary information? _____

8. Great Traits

Every organism has certain characteristics or traits. An elephant's wrinkled skin and the long, narrow shape of a stringbean are examples of traits.

There are three organisms listed below. Use the letters in TRAIT to help you reveal five traits common to each organism.

Bony Fish

_ _ _ T _ _ _ _   side fins

_ _ _ _ _ _ R   water pressure organ

_ _ A _ _ _   body cover

_ I _ _ _   breathes

_ _ _ T _ _ _ _ _ _   backbone

Flower

_ _ T _ _ _   pollen grains

_ _ _ R _   contains ovules

_ _ _ A _ _   protects petals

_ I _ _ _ _   female organ

_ _ T _ _ _   produce colors

Paramecium

_ _ _ _ _ _ T   throatlike structure

_ R _ _ _ _   mouth, oral _____

_ A _ _ _ _ _   space

_ I _ _ _   aids movement

_ _ _ _ _ _ _ T _ _ _   method of reproduction

A Challenge: Use each scattered letter once to identify three different traits.

t   r   o   e   o   x   s   c   t   e
    h   l   a   u   p   e
                            r

Answers: _____, _____, and _____.

9. It's Too Crowded

A term or person's name related to genetics is hidden in a group of letters. Use the clue(s) to find and circle the term. Write the term in the space provided to the right of the clue(s).

		Clue(s)	Term or Name
1.	axlisuttontrate	Scientist	_____
2.	ochpelkgameteir	Reproductive cell	_____
3.	snailspeaswheatrye	Mendel's "subjects"	
4.	bromendelsmithke	Father of Genetics	
5.	firstthyposomestwo	F_1 generation	_____
6.	domoffspringreciv	The young	_____
7.	crossrecessivetrte	Weak gene	_____
8.	geneditydominant	Strong gene	_____
9.	probotraitypest	Wrinkled or smooth seeds	_____
10.	chanceprinicipla	Unpredictable event	_____
11.	paratiosgenoyarexp	One out of three or two out of three	_____
12.	conmpsquaretaiw	Punnet ____?____	_____
13.	niseerinhybridove	Two different genes for a certain trait	_____
14.	depnotpurescenttwo	Two of the same genes for a certain trait	_____
15.	generationceniboma	Organisms living at the same time	_____
16.	timheredityshorikag	Inheritance of traits	_____
17.	tallpeasgenetics	Study of heredity	_____
18.	yonesecondthirdas	F_2 generation	_____
19.	moddihybridgamet	Cross; two different sets of traits	_____
20.	monohybridniret	Cross; only one trait involved	_____

© 1995 by The Center for Applied Research in Education

Name _____ Date _____

10. Genetic Mini-Puzzlers

Use your creative thinking ability to solve the following five items. Flexible thinking is the key to uncovering the answers.

1. Someone once said, "Mendel, the Father of Genetics, produced an end in the middle." What do you think this meant?

   Answer: _____

2. Chromosomes are dark, threadlike particles of DNA and proteins located in the nucleus of a cell. They carry the code for the inherited characteristics of an organism. What, then, makes up some of a chromosome?

   Answer: _____

3. Jennifer, a fourth grade student, said her favorite "subject" in school was leisure time. Unfortunately, her science, math, and English classes prevented her from spending more time "taking life easy." They, in a genetic sense, were *dominating* her school day. Genetically speaking, what would her recreation time at school be considered?

   Answer: _____

4. X and Y chromosomes determine the sex of an organism. An organism with two X chromosomes is a female. An organism that has one X and one Y chromosome is a male. How many female organisms can be produced from the chromosomes located in the box?

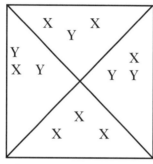

   Females: _____

5. The letter clues indicate what you inherit from your parents. Unscramble the answers to each letter clue and put them together to form a single word. Then use the word to complete the statement below.

   • This letter should "see" but it doesn't.

     _____

   • Two of these letters appear in the sound a snake makes.

     _____

   • This letter holds the eighteenth position.

     _____

   • This letter sounds like a hot or cold beverage.

     _____

   • Two of these letters appear in the largest artery in the human body.

     _____

   • Sounds like the peg that holds a golf ball.

     _____

According to the clues, I have inherited _____ from my parents.

Name _____ Date _____

11. Mr. D

A. Each box contains scattered letters. Unscramble them to spell the term described by the clue. Circle the remaining letters in each box.

1.
s	i	e	p
s	i	e	c

clue: group of organisms

term: _____

2.
f	i	s	w
s	o	s	l

clue: preserved remains

term: _____

3.
a	u	t	d	i
o	m	n	t	

clue: change in form

term: _____

4.
e	e	o	v
v	l	n	

clue: develop gradually

term: _____

5.
t	a	i	r	o	s
a	a	n	v	i	

clue: result of diversity

term: _____

6.
e	i	t	t
x	r	n	c

clue: no longer existing

term: _____

B. Unscramble the six circled letters to spell the name of the man who developed the theory of evolution.

The man is __ __ __ __ __ __

C. Use the letters scattered around the boat to spell *Darwin* as many times as you can. You may use each letter once.

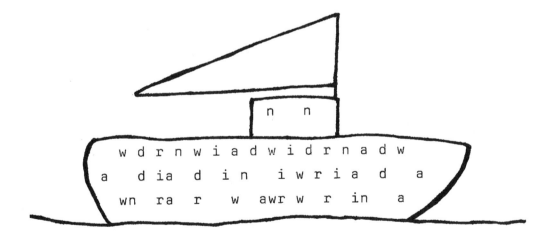

How many spellings did you get? _____

D. *Add* the number of times *Darwin* appears in Item C to number 12. Then subtract 14 from the total. Now you have the number of years Darwin's voyage on the HMS Beagle lasted. He collected animals, plants, and fossils on his voyage.

The number of years was _____

12. Scattered Fragments

There are 15 word fragments in the puzzle that complete each word related to evolution listed below the puzzle. Shade in each word fragment. Fragments may be up, down, forward, backward and diagonal. Then spell the complete word by writing the fragment in the space provided. Finally, unscramble the unshaded letters in the puzzle to reveal the answer to the mystery question.

P	L	A	I	K	J	N	R
A	C	V	M	A	G	O	I
T	E	R	N	R	M	I	V
U	A	G	A	S	A	T	N
M	E	D	■	U	L	A	E
S	T	S	G	R	S	L	T
E	N	E	L	N	I	S	E
I	E	A	C	I	E	P	A
T	M	T	N	T	S	T	B

1. _____ tion

2. _____ del

3. ch _____

4. fos _____

5. _____ me

6. _____ ants

7. _____ vive

8. adapt _____

9. _____ ualism

10. fit _____

11. _____ dence

12. exti _____

13. _____ onment

14. ani _____

15. _____ nes

Mystery Question: In the early 1800's, a French biologist developed some theories about evolution based on anatomy. What was his name?

His name was __ __ __ __   __ __ __ __ __ __ __ __   de __ __ __ __ __ __ __

Name _____ Date _____

13. The Strong Ones

Darwin believed that organisms best adapted to their surroundings would continue to survive. This concept became known as natural selection or survival of the fittest.

    Use the letters in natural selection as the first, fourth or last letters to name a plant or animal currently thriving on Earth. *Example:* carnatio<u>n</u> (last letter), <u>n</u>ewt (first letter)

	Plant	Animal
N	_____	_____
A	_____	_____
T	_____	_____
U	_____	_____
R	_____	_____
A	_____	_____
L	_____	_____
S	_____	_____
E	_____	_____
L	_____	_____
E	_____	_____
C	_____	_____
T	_____	_____
I	_____	_____
O	_____	_____
N	_____	_____

14. Change Through Time

Fossils are preserved evidence of past life. Fossils provide clues about how some organisms have changed through time. A complete, well-preserved fossil allows a scientist to make accurate observations. Let's play amateur scientist and put a few organisms together.

The paired letters below represent pieces of 12 different organisms. Match three sets of two-paired letters to form the name of a six-lettered "fossil" organism. Use the clues to help you find the answers.

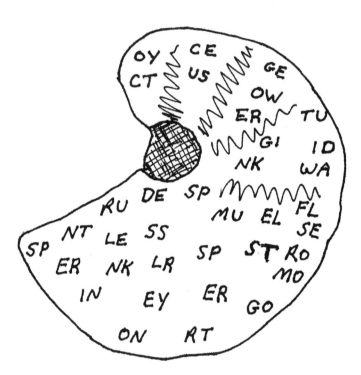

Clues	"Fossil" Organism
1. pearl	1.
2. web	2.
3. rose	3.
4. pores, water, porifera	4.
5. bug, beetle, or roach	5.
6. reptile, hard shell	6.
7. rat or mouse	7.
8. tree, rhymes with goose	8.
9. mollusk, rhymes with hustle	9.
10. primate, organ grinder	10.
11. mammal, tusks	11.
12. tree, native to China	12.

Name _____ Date _____

15. Evolution Cre-Eight-Ives

Here is a chance to tackle eight mini-problems and give your cerebral neurons a workout.

1. What does the illustration represent?

   Answer: _____

2. What does the illustration represent?

   Answer: _____

3. What does the illustration represent?

   Answer: _____

4. If Charles Darwin could pick one word from the list of 10 words, what selection would he make?

   1. tortoise   6. cormorant
   2. finch   7. penguin
   3. Galapagos   8. climate
   4. iguana   9. HMS Beagle
   5. natural   10. voyage

   Answer: _____

5. What does the illustration represent?

   Answer: _____

Evolution Cre-Eight-Ives
(con't)

6. What part of evolution indicates a score of nothing in tennis?

   Answer: _____

7. What does the illustration represent?

   ThEₒRy   THEORY   τHeOrY

   Answer: _____

8. Migrating organisms move into or out of a population. What animal is always in the middle of migration?

   Answer: _____

16. Mixed Up Plants

A. Unscramble the letters in parenthesis to reveal the plant structure. Write the unscrambled word in the appropriate space.

1. A carrot is an example of a (rotpato). _____

2. The (tihp) is the central area of a stem. _____

3. The layer of tissue between the xylem and the phloem is called the (mbamcui). _____

4. The (cluecit) is the waxy covering of a leaf. _____

5. A (otor) helps anchor a plant in the ground. _____

6. A (atoms) is an opening in the lower surface of a leaf's epidermis. _____

7. The outer, protective layer of a leaf is called the (imdseiper). _____

8. (Pomhel), a tubelike structure, can be found in a plant's root system. _____

9. One of two plant tissues that make up a vascular bundle is the (mxeyl). _____

10. A (lksat) connects a leaf to a stem. _____

11. (roCk) makes up the bark or outer covering of a tree. _____

12. The (cxotre) lies next to the cork layer. _____

B. Match the plant structure with its function. Write the name of the plant structure in the empty space. Use the first two letters *from the answer* in parenthesis to help you.

Plant Structure	Function
1. _____	1. Allows for gas exchange (st)
2. _____	2. Growth tissue of the stem (ca)
3. _____	3. Carries water through the plant (xy)
4. _____	4. Stores water and food (co)
5. _____	5. Prevents excessive water loss (cu)

C. Fill-In Challenge

Supply the missing letters to complete the following statement:

The Venus flytrap is a c _ r _ i _ o _ o _ s   p _ a _ t.

(two word answer)

17. It Begins With An S

Use the hints to help you identify the terms related to plants. All plant terms begin with the letter *s*.

It Begins With An S
(con't)

Across

1. A layer of cells in a leaf involved in gas exchange.
3. The pollen-bearing organ of a flower.
4. Tall, stout plant with a bright yellow flower; edible seeds.
5. An edible fruit from the gourd family.
9. Spores of a moss plant.
10. Slender growth supporting a flower or plant.
11. A very young plant or tree.
12. The Douglas fir.
13. Structures surrounding the petals of a flower.
14. The part of a pistil that receives the pollen.
15. Anything from the environment that elicits responses.

Down

1. A bud on a plant.
2. The ovule from which a plant may be reproduced.
3. A shoot on a plant.
4. Giant evergreen tree.
6. Cells that can develop into a new organism.
7. The substance in which plants grow.
8. The part of the pistil connecting the stigma to the ovary.
10. A type of moss.
11. Small openings in the underside of a leaf.
12. Energy from the sun.

18. Four Squares

Use the clues below each square to identify the terms that fit the puzzle. Answers may be forward, backward and upside down.

Puzzle #1

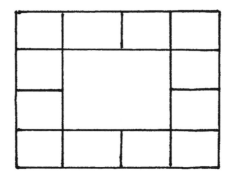

a. The planet where primitive life was thought to exist.

b. Small plants; coats rocks and tree trunks.

c. Acts to support the leaves and flowers of a plant.

d. Extraneous plant matter and other impurities on the surface of a pond.

Puzzle #2

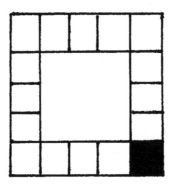

a. Simple water-dwelling plants that can make their own food.

b. Substance obtained from brown algae and used in making ice cream. *Hint:* Begins with an *a*, ends with an *n*.

c. A lacy, delicate-appearing plant that thrives in moist, shaded forests.

d. The reproductive unit of a conifer.

Name _____ Date _____

Four Squares
(con't)

Puzzle #3

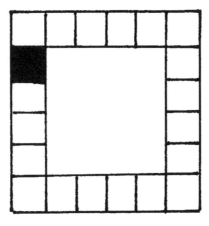

a. A collection of trees over a large area.

b. A plant must do this to increase in size.

c. Contains the soil where many plants grow.

d. A hot, dry area with few plants.

Puzzle #4

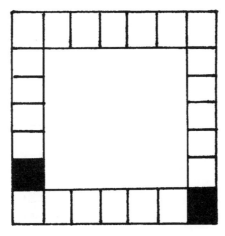

a. These tissues carry water and minerals from roots to leaves.

b. A substance found dissolved in water in the soil. Iron, for example, helps to keep a plant healthy.

c. These plant structures have a stalk and a blade.

d. A plant in which algae and fungi grow in partnership.

Name _____ Date _____

19. Vascular Plants

A vascular plant has a tubelike system of vessels for transporting materials to all plant cells. Use the letters in VASCULAR PLANTS ON EARTH to help you identify 21 different vascular plants.

1. V __ o __ e t

2. __ A __ s y

3. r __ S __

4. s __ r __ C e   tree

5. c __ U __   m __ s __   (two words)

6. t __ L __ p

7. c y __ A __

8. __ o R __ e t __ __ l

9. P __ n __   tree

10. p __ L __   tree

11. c __ d A __   tree

12. g __ N k __ __   tree

13. c __ c T __ s

14. __ r __ S

15. r __ __ w O __ d   tree

16. c __ __ N

17. __ E r __

18. __ A __   tree

19. __ R c __ __ d

20. T __ m a __ o

21. p __ a __ H

20. Fruit Mini-Puzzlers

According to Funk & Wagnalls, a fruit is a pulpy, usually edible mass covering the seeds of various plants and trees. Here are seven mini-puzzlers about fruit for you to solve.

1. How many fruits are hidden in the line of 25 letters:

    figfruitspeachtomatorange

    Answer: _____

2. How many figs are in the circle?

    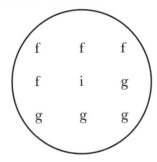

    Answer: _____

3. How many fruits begin with the letter *a*?

    Answer: _____

4. How would you like to receive a check for $50,000 from the fictitious company of Seedmore Brothers? All you have to do is name three different fruits that might be ingredients for their new product: ABC Fruit Punch.

    The name of each fruit ingredient must begin with the letter a, b or c. You can't use apple, apricot, berry or cherry. By the way, the fruit punch tastes terrible!

    Answer: A _____ B _____ C _____

5. Show how to describe or define a *fruit* by combining these three items: seeds, mature, and the letter *e*.

    Answer: _____

6. What does the illustration represent?

    Answer: _____

7. What would you get if you crossed an apricot with a fig?

    Answer: _____

21. Worms Are Invertebrates

There are several worms listed below. Match each worm with its description by placing the number of the worm next to the description. Then, in the diagram, shade in the spaces with the numbers you used. The unshaded portion will reveal the answer to the mystery question.

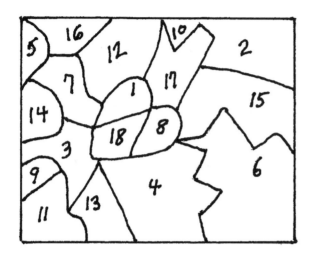

1. ribbon worm
2. trichina
3. planaria
4. mealworm
5. filaria worm
6. tapeworm
7. spiny-headed worm
8. pinworm
9. fluke

10. earthworm
11. feather duster worm
12. hookworm
13. leech
14. horsehair worm
15. pile worm
16. nematode
17. Ascaris
18. peanut worm

__ a. A parasitic worm found in the liver of a sheep.

__ b. A popular fish bait.

__ c. Known as the "cross-eyed" worm.

__ d. A parasitic plant worm.

__ e. A common roundworm of hogs and man.

__ f. Causes a disease known as trichinosis in man.

__ g. A parasitic worm consisting of many short sections.

__ h. A flat, segmented worm known to suck blood.

__ i. Beetle larva; small brownish worm; lives in grain products.

__ j. A worm known to cause elephantiasis.

__ k. A worm that lives around pier or wharf pilings.

__ l. This worm shows a display of "feathers."

__ m. A long, slender worm with a cylindrical body. It resembles the long hair of a certain mammal.

__ n. This parasitic worm is no friend to a bare-footed person.

__ o. This parasitic worm has hook-like structures around its head.

Mystery Question: What worm can cause severe damage to a dog's heart? _____

Name _____ Date _____

22. Land-Dwelling Invertebrates

It's tough to move around land without a backbone, but some organisms manage to survive quite well. Find and circle in the puzzle 20 of the 30 invertebrates listed below. Answers may be up, down, forward, backward and diagonal.

```
m  r  o  w  k  o  o  h  l  a  s  e  c  k
o  m  i  l  l  i  p  e  d  e  t  a  e  s
s  o  w  b  u  g  y  a  m  i  f  m  n  a
q  a  s  y  l  f  n  o  g  a  r  d  t  w
u  d  f  k  s  o  t  m  i  o  y  e  i  a
i  a  g  a  d  h  r  e  w  e  s  o  p  n
t  c  p  b  k  o  e  h  t  p  n  a  e  i
o  i  a  y  w  b  t  i  c  k  a  m  d  h
h  c  e  e  l  r  m  a  p  h  i  d  e  c
a  m  p  l  a  n  a  r  i  a  l  w  y  i
c  a  t  e  r  p  i  l  l  a  r  f  a  r
t  n  e  m  a  t  o  d  e  s  i  c  h  t
```

aphid	cicada	hookworm	moth	sowbug
bee	cricket	housefly	nematode	tapeworm
beetle	dragonfly	leech	planaria	tarantula
butterfly	earthworm	millipede	scorpion	tick
caterpillar	flea	mite	slug	trichina
centipede	grasshopper	mosquito	snail	wasp

Place the 20 invertebrates in their proper groupings.

Insects   Arachnids   Myriapods   Mollusks

_____   _____   _____   _____

_____   _____   _____   _____

_____

_____

_____

_____

Isopoda   Segmented Worms   Round Worms   Flatworms

_____   _____   _____   _____

                       _____   _____   _____

                                              _____

Name _____ Date _____

23. Insects Everywhere

Insects represent the largest group of animals on Earth. And, of course, all insects are invertebrates. Use the clues to identify 20 different insects. Write the name of the insect in the space to the right of the clues.

Clues   Insect

1. A honey of an invertebrate.   1. _____

2. Likes to chirp at night.   2. _____

3. An uninvited picnic guest.   3. _____

4. Always a lady.   4. _____

5. Prefers wood over most anything.   5. _____

6. Hates medicated pet collars.   6. _____

7. Has the name of a month in its name.   7. _____

8. Sounds like a piece of wood in motion.   8. _____

9. Goes from blade to blade.   9. _____

10. Sounds like an English outdoor game.   10. _____

11. "Man" looms large in this insect's name.   11. _____

12. A scavenger with a bad reputation.   12. _____

13. A stone makes up 68 percent of
    its name.   13. _____

14. An ear makes up 50 percent of its name.   14. _____

15. Can be found in some people's beds.   15. _____

16. Some wake up every 13 or 17 years.   16. _____

17. Even though it's half bee, it isn't a bee.   17. _____

18. You can't put a saddle on this fly.   18. _____

19. An Egyptian snake makes up 75 percent
    of this insect's name.   19. _____

20. The name suggests an insect who moves
    about in a clumsy manner or botches
    things up.   20. _____

What insect appears twice in the puzzle? _____

© 1995 by The Center for Applied Research in Education

24. Invertebrates At Sea

An invertebrate is an animal without a backbone. Find the letters that go with an *i* in each name of a different sea-living invertebrate. As you use a letter, circle it in the puzzle. Then fill in the blanks with the correct letters to spell the name of each organism. The matching responses are in the possible answers list.

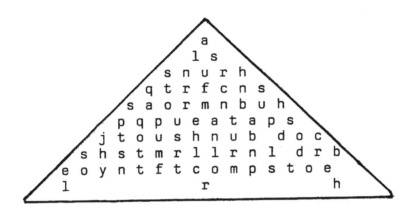

1. _ _ _ _ _ _ i _ _

2. _ _ _ i _

3. _ _ _ _ _ _ i _ _

4. _ _ _ i _

5. Sea _ _ _ _ i _

6. _ _ _ _ i _ crab

7. _ _ _ i _ _

8. _ _ _ i _ coral

9. _ i _ _ _ _ worm

10. _ _ _ _ i _ _ _

11. _ _ _ _ _ _ i (plural)

12. i _ _ _ _ _ _

13. Sea _ _ _ i _ _

14. _ i _ _ _ _

15. _ _ i _ _ _

Possible Answers

sessile	shrimp	starfish	hermit
jellyfish	chiton	pelvic	silver
obelia	mantis	brain	ribbon
squid	hydroid	octopi	nereis
diatom	tunic	limpet	snail
nautilus	urchin	bristle	squirt
pelagic	filter	isopod	
binary	cheliped	aurelia	

Name _____ Date _____

25. Times Up!

Are you ready for a super challenge? All you have to do is solve the seven invertebrate mini-puzzlers in 15 minutes or less. If you fail, well,…

Item One: Use the letters in INVERTEBRATE to spell the names of *two* different invertebrates. You may move letters around but you can't use the same letter twice.

Answer: _____ and _____

Item Two: Show how to change invertebrate into vertebrate using only three letters.

Answer: _____

Item Three: Show how to change vertebrate into invertebrate using only three letters.

Answer: _____

Item Four: Write the names of three insects using one t, one i, one w, one v, two l's, two b's and seven e's. *Hint:* Think of cotton, honey, and a name that rhymes with needle.

Answer: _____, _____ and _____

Item Five: Write the names of two invertebrates with fish as part of their names. *Note:* They live in water but are not considered fish.

Answer: _____ and _____

Item Six: Unscramble the letters to reveal a two-word answer to this question.

A tuna has been referred to as "Chicken of the Sea." Why, then, shouldn't a tuna be considered a vertebrate?

Answer: If a tuna is the "Chicken of the Sea," then it has __ __ __ __ __ __ __ __ __ __ (two words)

Item Seven: How many energetic worms do you count?

Answer: _____

© 1995 by The Center for Applied Research in Education

26. Vertebrate Equipment

A. Vertebrates have a backbone. Most of them have four limbs, a bony skeleton, and a brain housed inside a skull. Match the body structure on the left with the body region on the right. Place the letter of the body region in the space to the left of the number.

Body Structure

___ 1. humerus

___ 2. cerebellum

___ 3. femur

___ 4. optic lobe

___ 5. radius

___ 6. mandible

___ 7. tibia

___ 8. cerebrum

___ 9. maxilla

___ 10. medulla

Body Region

a. brain

b. bone, lower limb

c. bone, upper limb

d. bone, head

B. Place each of the 11 structures on the matching vertebrate sketches in the approximate location where it can be found. A structure may appear on more than one vertebrate sketch. Use the first or first and second letters of the structure to label the sketch. The first one is done for you.

Body Structures for Labeling the Sketches

1. caudal fin

2. operculum

3. tympanum

4. pectoral fin

5. nictitating membrane

6. crop

7. syrinx

8. femur

9. sternum

10. ulna

11. patella

Name _____ Date _____

Vertebrate Equipment
(con't)

Fish

Bird

Frog

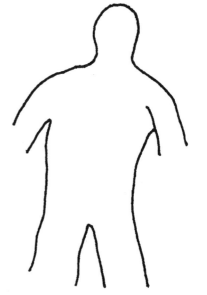

Man

Name _____ Date _____

27. Half and Half

Animals with backbones roam everywhere in this puzzle. The names of 20 vertebrates can be found in the two triangles below. The names are separated in half. The first half of a name appears in Triangle A and the second half is in Triangle B. Find both halves; then fill in the spaces under the triangles. PLACE THE NAMES IN ALPHABETICAL ORDER.

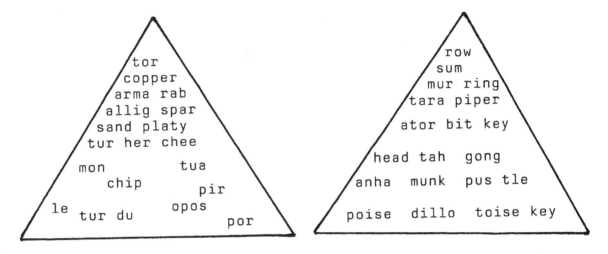

Triangle A   Triangle B

First Half of Name	Second Half of Name	Complete Name
1.	1.	1.
2.	2.	2.
3.	3.	3.
4.	4.	4.
5.	5.	5.
6.	6.	6.
7.	7.	7.
8.	8.	8.
9.	9.	9.
10.	10.	10.

Half and Half
(con't)

First Half of Name	Second Half of Name	Complete Name
11.	11.	11.
12.	12.	12.
13.	13.	13.
14.	14.	14.
15.	15.	15.
16.	16.	16.
17.	17.	17.
18.	18.	18.
19.	19.	19.
20.	20.	20.

Bonus

If you connect Triangle A and Triangle B at their bases, they would form a certain geometrical shape. The term is used to describe a baseball field. What vertebrate has a series of these patterns on its body?

Answer: _____

28. Enter the Mammal

There are 19 scrambled names of mammals. As you unscramble each name, write the name in the space to the right of the scrambled letters. Then write the *third* letter of each name in the corresponding number in the box. Three letters are provided in the box to get you started. The correct responses will give you the clues to complete the four items below the puzzle.

1	2	3	4 h	5
6	7	8	9	10
11	12 f	■	13	14 h
15	16	17	18	19

Item #1: A mammal has __ __ __ __ __   __ __ __ __ __ __ __ __ __
                          5   12 11 9 3   10 4 18 15 6 7 13 2 8

__ __ __ __ __.
14 1 16 17 19

Use the letters in the numbered sections of the box to spell the answer.

Item #2: Look at Numbers 15 through 19 in the box. Use all the letters to reveal two mammals. You may use the letter *r* twice.

        Mammal #1 _____

        Mammal #2 _____

Item #3: Look at Numbers 1 through 5 in the box. Use the corresponding numbers to spell the name of a mammal.

        Mammal _____

Item #4: Use the corresponding letters to Numbers 7, 8, and 11 to expose the last mammal.

        Mammal _____

Enter the Mammal
(con't)

Scrambled Names of Mammals

1. hetheca _____

2. otocel _____

3. ntamer _____

4. Letter *h*

5. erab _____

6. ibatrb _____

7. rede _____

8. dtnoer _____

9. knusk _____

10. ocnroca _____

11. spmouso _____

12. Letter *f*

13. rsamteom _____

14. Letter *h*

15. lmeru _____

16. vrebae _____

17. refter _____

18. hlewa _____

19. bta _____

29. Mystery Vertebrates

Use the clues to locate and circle each of the 12 mystery vertebrates in the puzzle. Answers may be up, down, forward, backward and diagonal. Write the name of each vertebrate in the space to the right of the clues.

e	g	d	o	l	p	h	i	n	c
a	o	h	o	n	s	t	a	o	i
c	r	o	r	i	a	e	r	x	m
a	f	r	a	b	d	m	i	o	d
m	a	s	g	o	o	p	o	r	a
e	w	e	n	r	l	s	a	e	o
l	n	o	a	u	e	z	s	i	t
t	i	n	k	y	i	w	m	a	e
l	t	e	a	l	r	o	n	z	b
z	e	n	i	p	u	c	r	o	p

Clues   Mystery Vertebrate

1. White fish, cold water, heavily harvested (3 letters)   1. _____

2. Slim, runs quickly, has scales and claws (6 letters)   2. _____

3. Hops, has pouch, lives down under (8 letters)   3. _____

4. Water bird, has an "ant" in its name (9 letters)   4. _____

5. Water, dorsal fin, plays the role of Flipper (7 letters)   5. _____

6. Smallmouth, water, largemouth (3 letters)   6. _____

7. Flies, sonar, large ears (3 letters)   7. _____

8. Largest deer, antlers, forest (5 letters)   8. _____

9. King, Leo, appeared in the Wizard of Oz (4 letters)   9. _____

10. Warty skin, short-legged, hops (4 letters)   10. _____

11. Quills, tree, forest (9 letters)   11. _____

12. Batman's friend, red breast, feathers (5 letters)   12. _____

Name _____ Date _____

Mystery Vertebrates
(con't)

Answer the following items:

A. List the three water-loving mystery vertebrates that use their fins for movement.

    1. _____   2. _____   3. _____

B. List the three mystery vertebrates that rely on wings for motion.

    1. _____   2. _____   3. _____

C. List the six mystery vertebrates that use limbs to move about.

    1. _____   2. _____   3. _____

    4. _____   5. _____   6. _____

Name _____ Date _____

30. What Is It?

Use your creative thinking ability to find answers to each of the following items:

1. What six-legged creature is hiding in coelacanth?

Answer:

2. What biblical vessel is part of a shark?

Answer:

3. What rodent "lives" in tuatara?

Answer:

4. What bone is part of a bird?

Answer:

5. What mammal can be made from a gun? (*Hint:* A three-lettered answer)

Answer:

6. What fish breathing structure is part of an alligator?

Answer:

7. What volcanic material can be found in a brown thrasher? (*Note:* The brown thrasher is a bird.)

Answer:

8. What space agency is tucked away in a pheasant?

Answer:

9. What part of a heron shows exceptional courage?

Answer:

10. What part of an armadillo belongs to the parsley family?

Answer:

11. What part of a cottontail rabbit weighs the most?

Answer:

12. What negative word makes up one half of a badger?

Answer:

13. What plaything helps keep a coyote happy?

Answer:

14. What is the sharpest part of a porcupine?

Answer:

15. What part of a weasel suggests freedom from physical discomfort?

Answer:

16. What tissue covers most of a skink?

Answer:

17. What fish helps make up a crocodile?

Answer:

18. What keeps a newt fresh?

Answer:

19. What is the smallest living organism found on an elephant?

Answer:

20. What is not truthful about a collie dog?

Answer:

31. Skull Session

Combine two, three or four scattered letter groups together to spell 12 different bones in the skull.

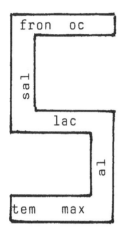 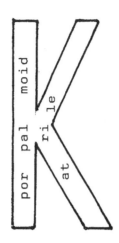 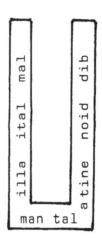 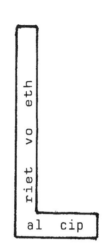 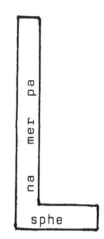

1. List the six cranial bones in ALPHABETICAL ORDER.

    1.

    2.

    3.

    4.

    5.

    6.

2. List the six facial bones in ALPHABETICAL ORDER.

    1.

    2.

    3.

    4.

    5.

    6.

3. What two facial bones are needed for chewing, tearing, and grinding food?

    1.

    2.

4. What does the lacrimal gland located near the lacrimal bone produce?

    Answer:

5. What skull bone would be the first to meet the impact of a hard blow to the back of the skull?

    Answer:

32. Limb, Hand, and Foot Bones

Bones of the upper and lower limbs, hands, and foot fit the puzzle. Use the letters in the puzzle as a guide.

Use the clues to help you fill in the missing letters. The answers are related to limbs, hands, and the foot.

Clues

L _ _ _ _ _ _ _ _	Joins bone to bone
_ _ I _	Another name for tibia
M _ _ _ _ _ _	Tissue that contracts
B _ _ _	Connective tissue
S _ _ _	Covers bone, muscle, and tissue
_ H _ _ _	First digit
_ A _ _	Under part
_ N _ _ _ _ _	First joint lump
_ _ D _ _	First finger or forefinger
F _ _ _ _ _	Cause of athlete's foot
_ _ _ _ _ O _	Painful swelling
_ O _	Front end of bone
T _ _ _ _ _	Ankle bone

Name _____ Date _____

33. Bones in a Box

Use five letters in each box to spell the name of a bone located in the human body. Write the bone name in the space under the box. Circle the remaining letter in the box.

1.
p	b	n
e	s	i

_____

2.
s	t	a
a	i	l

_____

3.
i	u	i
s	l	m

_____

4.
b	i	p
c	u	r

_____

Unscramble the four circled letters to answer this question: What bones can be true or false?

Answer: _____

Identify the five scattered bones. Write the name of the bone in the space to the right of the sketch.

1.

_____

2.

_____

3.

_____

4.

_____

5.

_____

If you correctly identify the five scattered bones, you will be able to fit the answers in the puzzle below.

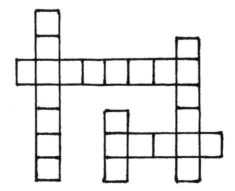

Bones in a Box
(con't)

Here are three mini-puzzlers. Do you know what they all have in common?

a.

2 - 15 - 14 - 5 - 19

b.

c.

34. Mixed Bag of Bones

Complete the sentences below with the letters that spell the correct bone names. Then transfer the numbered letters to the BIG BONE BONUS puzzle. The completed puzzle will provide the answer to the BIG BONE BONUS question.

1. The C __ __ __ __ __ __ protects the brain.
                  3

2. The __ __ m __ __ is the largest bone in the body.
            14

3. The tibia is the __ h __ __ b __ __ __.
                      1   7

4. The r __ __ __ __ __ and __ __ n __ make up the forearm.
           8   16   4

5. The __ __ m __ __ __ __ is the upper arm bone.
                17

6. The __ __ t __ __ __ __ is the kneecap.
         6   5

7. The sternum is the __ r __ __ __ t __ __ __ __.
                        9

8. The __ __ p __ __ __ __   __ r __ __ __ __ __ is part of the sternum.
             11   12

9. The m __ __ __ i __ __ __ is the lower jaw.
          13   10

10. The largest __ n __ __ __ bone is the calcaneus.
                  2   15

Big Bone Bonus Question: What is the meaning of the puzzle words? *Hint:* Read from top to bottom.

Name _____ Date _____

Mixed Bag of Bones
(con't)

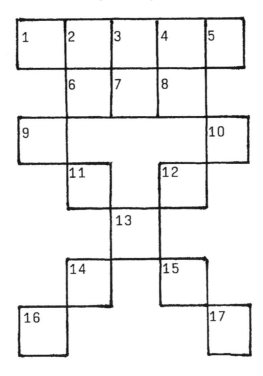

Count the letters in the bone sketch. How many times can you spell BONE?

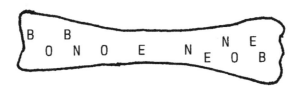

Answer: _____

35. Bones Galore!

Use the clues in the right hand margin to identify each bone. Place the letters that spell each bone name in the empty spaces to the right of the number.

Clues

1. _ _ _ _ _ _ _   Five fused vertebrae

2. _ _ _ _ _ _ _ _   Shoulder blade

3. _ _ _ _ _ _   Bone in nasal area

4. _ _ _ _ _ _ _ _   Collarbone

5. _ _ _ _ _ _   Tailbone

6. _ _ _ _ _ _   Lower vertebra

7. _ _ _ _ _ _ _ _   Vertebrae between cervical and lumbar

8. _ _ _ _ _ _ _   Neck vertebra

9. _ _ _ _ _   One of first two neck vertebrae

10. _ _ _ _ _ _ _ _ _   Upper part of sternum

11. _ _ _ _ _ _ _ _ _   Finger and toe bones

12. _ _ _ _ _ _ _ _ _ _ Bones between the wrist and fingers

13. _ _ _ _   Forearm bone

14. _ _ _ _ _ _ _   Kneecap

15. _ _ _ _ _ _ _ _   Inferior part of coxal bone

16. _ _ _ _ _ _ _   Upper jaw

17. _ _ _ _ _ _ _ _ _   Cheekbone

18. _ _ _ _ _ _ _   Bone next to tibia

19. _ _ _ _ _ _ _ _ _   Helps form sides and base of cranium

20. _ _ _ _ _ _   Forearm bone

What Do You Think?

A farmer discovered hundreds of fossilized vertebrae in his orchard. He decided to convert the orchard into a theme park. What do you think he planned to name it?

Answer: _____

What Do You Think?

Mrs. Tarsal introduced her husband, John Tarsal, to her boss, Carla Carpal. They shook hands. What do you think Mr. Tarsal did?

Answer: _____

36. ABC's of Human Body Structures

There are 26 human body structures hidden in the puzzle. Each structure begins with a different letter of the alphabet. Find and circle each structure in the puzzle. Answers may be up, down, forward, backward and diagonal. List each structure in the appropriate space below.

```
w  a  d  i  o  h  p  i  x  s  x  m  v  e  v  a
r  z  y  g  o  m  a  t  i  c  a  u  l  n  a  c
i  m  u  s  c  l  e  c  l  k  s  n  j  z  l  a
s  e  b  a  y  i  r  a  n  l  u  r  o  y  v  r
t  n  o  d  n  e  t  e  o  o  i  e  i  g  e  t
a  z  n  v  q  i  e  y  z  y  d  t  n  o  n  i
x  q  e  s  p  a  n  c  r  e  a  s  t  m  e  l
i  t  l  i  g  a  m  e  n  t  r  y  e  a  r  a
a  i  c  h  u  m  e  r  u  s  t  o  o  f  v  g
i  c  e  l  b  o  w  r  o  s  i  c  n  i  e  e
o  a  r  y  g  s  p  e  c  i  r  d  a  u  q  x
n  o  i  l  g  n  a  g  e  o  l  a  m  r  e  d
```

a_____ skeleton (2 words)   n _____

b _____   o _____

c_____   p _____

d _____   q _____

e_____   r _____

f _____   s _____

g _____   t _____

h _____   u _____

i_____   v _____

j_____   w _____

k _____   x _____ process (2 words)

l_____   y _____

m_____   z _____ arch (2 words)

37. Support and Movement

Use the clues to help you complete the crossword puzzle.

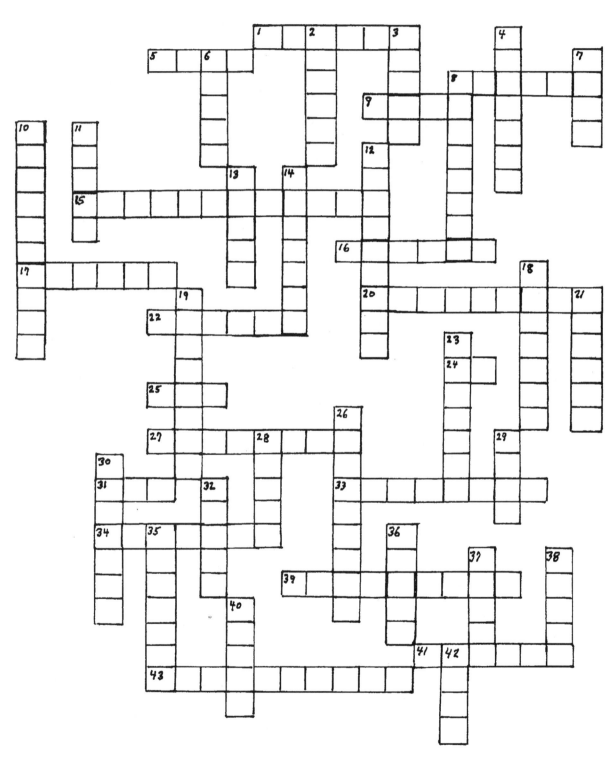

Name _____ Date _____

Support and Movement
(con't)

Across

1. Houses the hip bone
5. Bones protecting the heart and lungs
8. A wrist bone
9. A hinge joint protected by the patella
15. Shoulder, hip, arm and leg bones make up this skeleton
16. A partner to the shinbone
17. Attaches muscles to bones
20. Inflammation of the joints
22. A forearm bone
24. The chemical symbol for a bone-building element
25. Edge of the pelvis
27. The collar bone
31. An upper limb
33. Vertebrae located between the cervical and lumbar
34. Lowest structure of the hipbone
39. Finger and toe bones
41. Soft tissue that fills spaces in spongy bone
43. Lies in front of the tarsal bones

Down

2. Lower body vertebrae
3. The bony column made up of 33 vertebrae
4. Foot bones
6. Hinged and held together by ligaments
7. The larger of the two forearm bones
8. Neck vertebrae
10. Thin, tough membrane covering a bone
11. Skull, rib cage, and backbone make up this skeleton
12. Tough, flexible tissue
13. The shinbone
14. An upper arm bone
18. The breastbone
19. Lower jaw
21. A triangular-shaped bone in the pelvis
23. The shoulder blade
26. Small bones protecting the nerve cord
28. The protecting part of the hip bone
29. Another name for tibia
30. Upper jaw bone
32. Where two bones meet
35. Another name for the skull
36. Middle section of a long bone
37. Largest bone in the body
38. The joint between the forearm and upper arm
40. The first bone in the neck
42. The second neckbone

38. Which Way Out of the Bone Maze?

Begin at the *Entrance* of the puzzle. Follow each of the numbered clues in order. As you read each clue, write the name of the bone as indicated in the blanks. Some of the bones are already present in the puzzle. If you complete the maze correctly, you will find your way out of the maze. Will the *Exit* be A, B, C, D, E, or F?

Clues

1. A large leg bone belongs near the *Entrance.*

2. The bone found next to the shin bone goes south.

3. The next bone, lower jaw, lies east and west.

4. The five-lettered shin bone crosses the lower jaw.

5. The skull bone connects to the west end of the lower jaw. It is backwards and lies north and south.

6. The shoulder blade connects to the skull bone. It lies east and west.

7. The last letter of the shoulder blade is "a." This is the first letter of the first bone in the neck.

8. The collar bone ends at Point B. Sorry. This is a blind alley.

9. Keep heading south. The last letter of the first bone in the neck is "s." "S" is the last letter of the upper arm bone which is spelled backwards.

10. Due south lies the "floating bone" found inside the head. It ends in "oid."

11. Go to "p" in xiphoid. It's a phalanx of the fingers or toes. Point F is another blind alley.

12. The "1" in Number 11 above is the first letter of the vertebrae between the cervical and thoracic vertebrae. Once again, Point E turns out to be another blind alley.

13. Now move over to ribs spelled backwards *sbir.* "S" going south is the first letter of the bone that anchors the spine to the pelvis. "S" going north is the first letter of the breastbone.

14. The bone that lies east and west pointing to Exit D is the tailbone. You guessed it: another dead end. And yes, this bone is spelled backwards.

15. Now that leaves either Point A or Point C. Which is it? Go to allixam (maxilla spelled backwards). The neck vertebra fits the north/south pattern. Sorry. Point A represents a solid wall; no opening here. The vertebrae found between the cervical and lumbar nicely fills the blanks running east and west.

16. The name of the second neckbone fits in the last three spaces. Point C is the exit. You're out of the maze.

Congratulations

Which Way Out of the Bone Maze?
(con't)

Entrance

A

a l l i x a m

C

s
u
i
d
a

p
a
t
e
l
l
a

B

s b i r

s
a
c
r
u
m

l
i
u l n a
m

D

x i p h o i d

E

l

N

W ← → E

S

F

39. Digestion, Respiration, and Reproduction

There are 40 terms listed below the puzzle. Find and circle 30 of the terms in the puzzle. Terms may be up, down, forward, backward and diagonal.

```
s  a  s  e  m  y  z  n  e  p  h  s  u  r  e  t  u
e  t  o  x  a  s  v  m  c  o  a  e  o  w  g  o  s
l  i  a  y  o  w  y  p  h  a  y  i  l  m  g  p  a
i  z  s  r  t  h  n  k  y  f  r  m  r  t  e  x  m
t  p  g  e  c  s  b  r  o  i  a  u  j  r  o  a  g
r  e  n  c  q  h  a  o  f  l  l  t  m  e  n  l  t
e  n  u  t  x  l  d  l  a  o  l  o  x  y  g  e  n
f  i  l  u  o  v  e  e  i  e  i  r  w  t  s  p  a
s  t  o  m  a  c  h  y  l  v  p  c  m  u  e  l  m
a  s  i  t  e  p  t  t  a  l  a  s  t  h  m  a  k
o  e  o  l  m  d  u  r  r  a  c  e  e  s  o  c  i
p  t  a  e  l  u  o  e  y  n  f  m  s  e  l  e  a
b  n  l  c  v  i  m  b  n  s  a  o  t  a  t  n  p
x  i  m  y  e  o  v  u  x  i  v  r  e  c  f  t  e
b  r  s  u  c  u  m  p  s  p  e  p  s  i  n  a  p
```

anus	embryo	molar	rectum
alveoli	enzymes	mouth	saliva
asthma	feces	mucus	scrotum
bile	fertile	ovaries	sperm
breathe	fetus	oxygen	starch
bronchi	food	pancreas	stomach
capillary	intestine	pepsin	testes
cervix	larynx	pharynx	trachea
chyme	liver	placenta	uterus
egg	lungs	puberty	villi

Here are definitions or descriptions for 10 terms found in the puzzle. Write the matching term in the appropriate space.

1. A glandular secretion. _____
2. Capable of reproduction. _____
3. The organ of voice. _____
4. Air cells of the lungs. _____
5. A grinding tooth. _____
6. An enzyme of gastric juice. _____
7. A liquid mixture of partially digested food. _____
8. A liver secretion. _____
9. A major organ of digestion. _____
10. Creates difficulty in breathing. _____

Name _____ Date _____

40. Staying in Circulation

Write the term that best fits each description in the space provided. Then find the answer in the puzzle and draw a line through it.

1. The largest artery of the heart. _____

2. The mammal heart has _____ chambers.

3. Blood vessels have a middle layer of _____ muscle.

4. Coronary _____ empty the blood into the right _____ of the heart.

5. Blood is forced into the _____ each time the _____ contract.

6. Veins have cuplike _____ that prevent the backflow of blood.

7. _____ is the movement of molecules from an area of greater concentration to an area of lesser concentration.

8. Blood from the body enters the right atrium from the _____ veins.

9. _____ circulation refers to the pathway of blood between lungs and heart.

10. The _____ artery leads to the head.

11. A universal donor carries _____ _____ blood.

12. _____ are microscopic threads that help blood clot.

13. _____ _____ cells are produced in the spleen.

14. _____ transports oxygen to tissues.

15. _____ is about 90 percent water.

16. _____ _____ cells make up 44 percent of the blood.

17. Red blood cells pass through the smallest _____ in single file.

18. Blood travels through the pulmonary artery to the _____.

19. _____ is a group of similar cells performing a particular function.

20. An _____ is a protein material in blood which fights infection by destroying microbes.

Staying in Circulation
(con't)

PLASMA
VENA CAVA
CLOT
ANTIBODY
SYSTOLE
SEPTUM
LUNGS
VENTRICLES
PULMONARY
TYPE O
CAROTID
WHITE BLOOD
CAPILLARIES
HEMOGLOBIN
AORTA
FOUR
VEINS
ROUGH
ATRIUM
ORGAN
SKIN
DIASTOLE
OXYGEN

Look at the puzzle. If you have completed it correctly, you will be able to answer the following items correctly:

1. All the answers connect, do not connect (circle one) with each other.

2. There are 7, 9, or 10 (circle one) answers that occur in a vertical pattern.

3. There are 12, 13, or 14 (circle one) answers that occur in a horizontal pattern.

41. Twenty Broken Health Terms

There are twenty health terms listed below the puzzle. Unfortunately, the letters of each term need to be connected with a line. The first one is done for you. Lines *must NOT* cross anywhere in the puzzle.

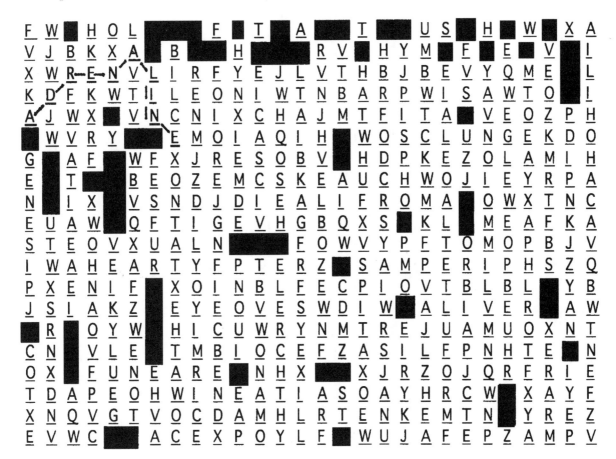

adrenaline	bronchi	hemophilia	pituitary
amylase	endocrine	holistic	remission
arthritis	enzyme	interferon	symptom
benign	genetic	lymph	thymus
biopsy	glaucoma	nutrient	vaccine

42. The ABC's of Infectious Disease

Shade in six terms beginning with the *letter a* that are related in some way to infectious diseases. Then write the term in the space to the right of the puzzle. Do the same for six terms beginning with the *letters b and c*. Terms may be up, down, forward, backward and diagonal.

Letter a

1. _____ dysentery
2. _____
3. _____
4. _____ immunity
5. _____ foot
6. _____

Letter b

1. _____
2. _____
3. _____ plague
4. _____
5. _____
6. _____

Letter c

1. _____
2. _____
3. _____
4. _____ pox
5. _____
6. _____

What might the shaded areas around the body represent? The shaded areas might represent a

_____ .

43. Word Within a Word

Find and circle a word within each listed word below that relates to good health. The first one is done for you.

1. s(pill)ed
2. restaurant
3. buckshot
4. telescope
5. scared
6. recommend
7. fungus
8. refreshment
9. disease
10. speaker

11. deliver
12. stairway
13. buckskin
14. father
15. generic
16. permineralize
17. Milky Way
18. reminder
19. nobody
20. swell

Briefly describe how the following items work together to produce good health.

Items 18 and 19

Items 13 and 19

Finally, how do you think Item 15 relates to good health?

44. Five Letters

Five letters—a, e, i, o and h—make up one half or more of the letters necessary to spell the terms that identify each of the items below. Use the clues to help you reveal the terms.

Clues   Terms

1. well-being; absence of disease.   1. _____

2. disease; blackheads and pimples.   2. _____

3. heat unit; measure of energy.   3. _____

4. pathological body state; illness.   4. _____

5. to recognize a health problem.   5. _____

6. old age; mental deterioration.   6. _____

7. innermost; light-sensing part of the eye.   7. _____

8. liquid; salivary; mouth.   8. _____

9. reaction; feeling; mental state.   9. _____

10. thyroid; loss of iodine; swelling.   10. _____

11. chemical substance; bloodstream; e.g., insulin   11. _____

12. colored structure; eye; contains pupil.   12. _____

13. used to treat a disease or disorder.   13. _____

14. extremely fat; overweight.   14. _____

15. body tissues; fluid; swelling.   15. _____

Now place the answers in alphabetical order.

1. _____   6. _____   11. _____

2. _____   7. _____   12. _____

3. _____   8. _____   13. _____

4. _____   9. _____   14. _____

5. _____   10. _____   15. _____

List a word that describes how numbers 5 and 7 are alike?

_____

List a word that describes how numbers 10 and 13 are alike?

_____

© 1995 by The Center for Applied Research in Education

Name _____ Date _____

45. Follow the Path

Answer the 12 items correctly and you'll travel smoothly through the puzzle. Place the letters to each item in the puzzle spaces. The last letter of each answer will be the first letter for the next response. Begin at START and continue until you reach the FINISH.

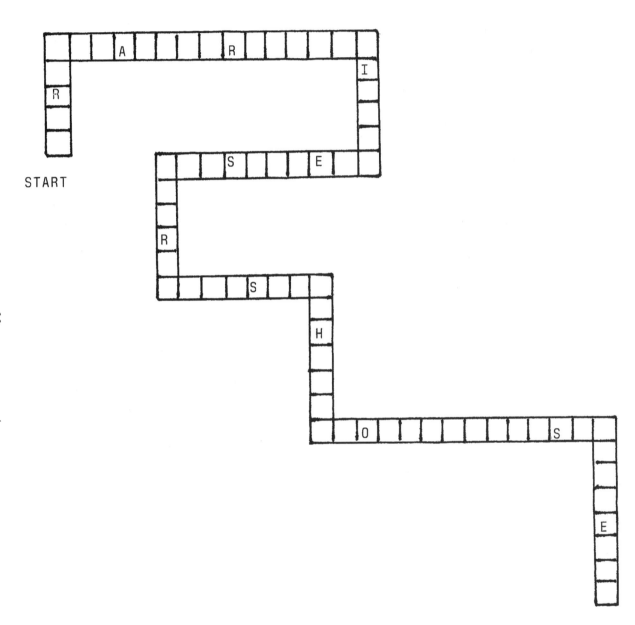

START

FINISH

Follow the Path
(con't)

Items

1. A disease causing germ.
2. Stretched or torn ligaments or tendons near a joint.
3. A nerve cell.
4. An addictive substance found in tobacco.
5. The outermost layer of skin.
6. Salivary glands secrete this liquid.
7. Carries blood from the heart.
8. Another word for perspiration.
9. The gland that produces thyroxine.
10. The proper amount of a drug.
11. A breathing disorder.
12. Memory loss.

Name _____ Date _____

46. Biotic Beings

Ecology is the study of relationships between organisms and their environments. Living organisms, plants, and animals make up the biotic factors in various environments.

A. There are 15 animals and five plants in the four shapes below. Find and list them under their proper headings.

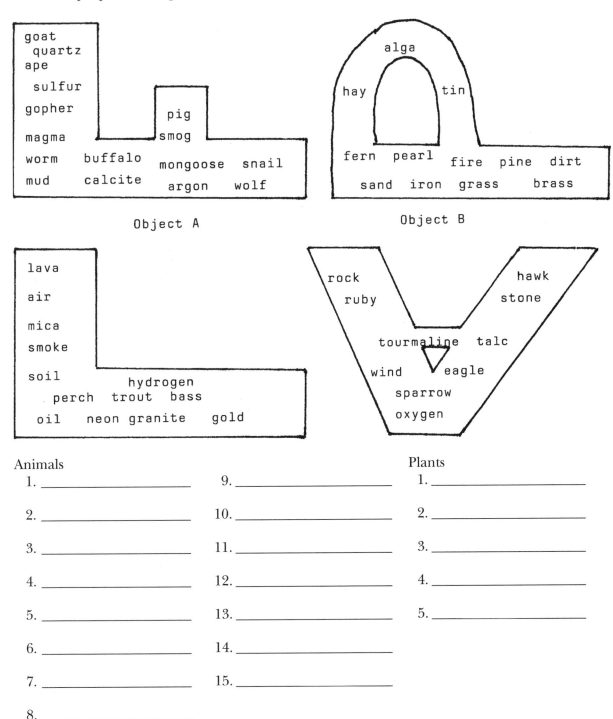

Object A

Object B

Animals

1. _____ 9. _____

2. _____ 10. _____

3. _____ 11. _____

4. _____ 12. _____

5. _____ 13. _____

6. _____ 14. _____

7. _____ 15. _____

8. _____

Plants

1. _____

2. _____

3. _____

4. _____

5. _____

Biotic Beings
(cont't)

B. Examine each object carefully. Use your imagination and feel free to be creative. Now answer these items:

   1. What is the relationship between Object A and its organisms?

      Answer: _____

   2. What is the relationship between Object B and its organisms?

      Answer: _____

   3. What is the relationship between Object C and its organisms?

      Answer: _____

   4. What is the relationship between Object D and its organisms?

      Answer: _____

C. Fill in the spaces with letters identifying "biotic beings." The first one is done for you. Use the clues to help you.

	Clues
B i r d s	Atmospheric environment
I _ _ _ _ _ _	Six-legged creatures
_ O _ _ _ _ _	Preserved organisms from the past
T _ _ _ _	Big part of forest
_ _ _ I _ _ _ _	Cone-bearing trees
C _ _ _	Source of hydrocarbons

Name _____ Date _____

47. Abiotic Adventure

Abiotic factors are the nonliving things in the environment. Identify the following 26 abiotic factors using a different letter of the alphabet as the first letter in the word. You will be given one clue to help you identify the factors.

Abiotic Factors	Clue	Abiotic Factor	Clue
A _____	Atmosphere	N _____	Gas
B _____	Sleep	O _____	Gas
C _____	Soil	P _____	Hockey
D _____	Particles	Q _____	Quartz
E _____	Gemstone	R _____	Stone
F _____	Burn	S _____	Dirt
G _____	Transparent	T _____	Furniture
H _____	Gas	U _____	Rain
I _____	Frozen	V _____	Music
J _____	Green	W _____	Liquid
K _____	Pot	X _____	Music
L _____	Sun	Y _____	Weaving
M _____	Volcano	Z _____	Metal

Bonus

Use the letters in ABIOTIC to spell three, three-lettered abiotic factors. You may use a letter more than once. *Hint:* One word rhymes with *rib,* one with *spot,* and one with *pit.*

Answers: _____, _____, and _____.

48. Ecosystem Wordsearch

An ecosystem is all the living and nonliving parts of an environment. There are 15 term descriptions related to the ecosystem below the puzzle. The first letter of the term is provided to help you get started. Find and circle each term in the puzzle. Then write the term next to the matching description. Terms may be up, down, forward, backward, and diagonal.

```
s   n   e   f   c   p   r   e   d   a   t   o   r   y
u   i   t   o   r   a   h   f   u   l   a   t   e   r
c   a   i   o   b   c   e   y   p   b   e   r   c   e
c   h   s   d   i   c   h   w   i   l   p   k   o   c
e   c   a   n   o   u   z   o   c   m   o   i   l   u
s   d   r   e   t   g   t   y   s   k   v   k   o   d
s   o   a   b   i   i   c   a   p   t   a   b   g   o
i   o   p   x   c   o   m   m   u   n   i   t   y   r
o   f   m   s   r   e   m   u   s   n   o   c   a   p
n   e   n   e   r   g   y   b   e   w   d   o   o   f
```

Terms

1. b_____
2. a_____
3. c_____
4. e_____
5. n _____
6. s _____
7. p _____
8. p _____
9. p _____
10. f_____ c _____
11. h _____
12. c_____
13. f_____ w _____
14. c_____
15. p _____

Description

1. Living organisms
2. Nonliving parts of the ecosystem
3. All the biotic factors within a certain area.
4. Study of the relationship between organisms and their environment.
5. A species' role within a community
6. A gradual, orderly change of species in a community over time
7. Organism that lives in or on a host at the host's expense
8. An organism which makes its own food
9. An organism being preyed upon by an animal
10. The passage of energy and materials through a community
11. Organism from which a parasite benefits
12. A series of events or activities
13. The combining and overlapping of food chains
14. Organisms that secure food by eating other organisms
15. Animal that preys on another organism

Ecosystem Wordsearch
(con't)

Mini-Puzzler #1 Refer to Puzzle Terms

Decomposers in an ecosystem feed on dead organisms.

$\underset{1}{\_} \ \underset{2}{\_} \ \underset{12}{\_} \ \_ \ \underset{4}{\_} \ \_ \ \_ \ \underset{2}{\_}$ form one group of decomposers. The

numbers corresponding to the *first* letters of the term answers 1, 2, 12, and 4 are provided. (Number 2 appears twice). You must supply the three missing letters to expose the answer.

Mini-Puzzler #2

The place where an organism lives is its habitat. Find the name of an organism hiding in the word HABITAT. Then unscramble four of the eight letters—r i v a m o e c—to reveal the organism's habitat.

Organism _____

Organism's Habitat _____

49. Mixed-Up Biomes

A. A biome is a community characterized by the same major life forms. Six land forms are featured below. There are five organisms included in each biome. Two climatic factors—rainfall and temperature—determine the type of land biome. However, there is a problem: Some of the organisms are in the wrong biome. Draw a line through the organisms that *do not* belong in each biome.

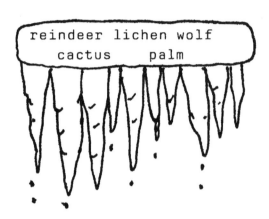

Tundra
Climate: freezing

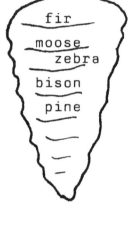

Coniferous Forest
Climate: cold winter,
short summers

Deciduous Forest
Climate: cold winters,
warm summers

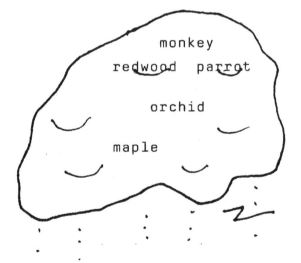

Tropical Rain Forest
Climate: rainy and warm

Name _____ Date _____

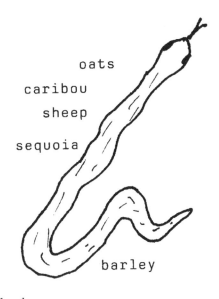

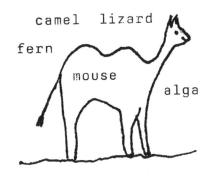

oats
caribou
sheep
sequoia
barley

camel lizard
fern
mouse
alga

Grasslands
Climate: cold winters;
hot, dry summers

Desert
Climate: hot days, cold nights;
sparse rainfall

B. List the *lined out* organisms from Part A in the spaces below. *Hint:* There are 12 of them.

1.   7.
2.   8.
3.   9.
4.   10.
5.   11.
6.   12.

C. Now separate the organisms from Part B into two groups—plants and animals. *Hint:* There are seven plants and five animals.

Plants   Animals
1.   1.
2.   2.
3.   3.
4.   4.
5.   5.
6.
7.

D. List two animals from Part C that live in Africa.

1.

2.

E. Look at all five biomes. Select the largest and smallest plant and animal organisms.

Plants   Animals
Largest: _____   Largest: _____
Smallest: _____   Smallest: _____

50. Water Biomes

A. Two major water biomes are fresh water and salt water. There are 20 organisms hidden in the puzzle that live in these water biomes. *Draw a line* through the 10 salt water organisms and *circle* the 10 fresh water organisms. If an organism lives in both fresh and salt water, it will appear twice in the puzzle.

```
a  g  l  a  l  l  i  g  e  u  l  b  s
d  c  u  n  b  y  s  u  m  a  u  n  t
i  l  m  x  l  a  a  t  v  x  a  o  u
c  a  n  u  t  u  l  r  z  i  e  e  r
a  m  t  o  n  s  m  o  l  u  t  g  g
e  k  i  p  f  r  o  g  n  k  i  r  e
s  q  u  i  d  s  n  u  d  e  c  u  o
r  n  o  m  l  a  s  t  l  s  l  t  n
o  u  h  a  c  p  r  a  c  z  a  s  q
c  y  g  l  z  a  h  x  o  u  c  e  p
k  l  u  c  r  w  r  e  t  s  b  o  l
a  c  r  a  p  p  i  e  l  i  a  n  s
```

B. *List the 10 fresh water organisms in ALPHABETICAL ORDER.*

1. _____
2. _____
3. _____
4. _____
5. _____

6. _____
7. _____
8. _____
9. _____
10. _____

C. List two hard-shelled fresh water organisms that live on a muddy or sandy bottom.

1. _____
2. _____

D. List the 10 salt water organisms in ALPHABETICAL ORDER.

1. _____
2. _____
3. _____
4. _____
5. _____

6. _____
7. _____
8. _____
9. _____
10. _____

Water Biomes
(con't)

E. List four salt water organisms that are protected by a hard outer covering.

1. _____   3. _____

2. _____   4. _____

F. *Find The Mystery Word*

There is an area where fresh water meets and mixes with ocean water. An example would be a salt marsh or mud flat.

What is the name of this area? E_ __ __ U __ __ Y

Here are seven hints:

1. Letter E

2. Shore birds live here

3. The tide meets the river currents

4. Letter U

5. Algae grows along the shore

6. Rivers bring nutrients into the area

7. Letter Y

Last Hint: If you're having trouble completing the word, look for a pattern in the list of hints.

SECTION TWO

Physical Science

Name _____ Date _____

51. Energy Is Energy

How many of the following ten items can you solve? Let's find out.

1. Use the letters below to spell ENERGY. You may use each letter once. How many times does ENERGY appear?

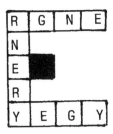

2. Unscramble the letters and number to form a type of energy.

    al + 10 + po + i + t

3. What kind of energy is this?

    <u>energy</u>
    the move

4. What is this?

5. What is this?

6. What is this?

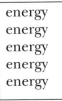

Energy Is Energy
(con't)

7. What would have to be done with ENERGY to produce something GREEN?

8. Spell ENERGY using five letters.

9. Three forms of energy fit the puzzle. *Authentic* rhymes with one term, *might* rhymes with one, and *sleet* rhymes with one.

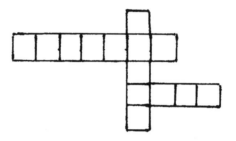

10. What does the sketch represent?

E ⟶ EN ⟶ ENE ⟶ ENER ⟶

⟶ ENERG ⟶ ENERGY

52. Six Types

A. There are six types of energy below, one energy type per unit. Use the letters in each unit to spell the name of a type of energy. Place the name in the appropriate space below each unit.

1. c   e   l   a   n   c
    h   g   i   m   a   n

_____ (10 letters)

2.   a   t
     e   i   h

_____ (4 letters)

3. a   n   i   d
   t   n   a   r

_____ (7 letters)

4. t   c   r   u
   a   n   e   l

_____ (7 letters)

5. c   h   i   l   e
   m   l   i   c   a

_____ (8 letters)

6. g   o   h   s
   n   u   d

_____ (5 letters)

B. Use the extra nine letters to spell the answer to the question: What is an example of electric energy?

Answer: __ __ __ __ __ __ __ __ __

C. Mini-Problem
What do these three ENERGY figures represent?

Answer:

Name _____ Date _____

53. Energy Is As Energy Does

Energy of motion is known as kinetic energy. All moving bodies have kinetic energy.

A. Circle the numbers of the moving bodies listed below.

1. pendulum		9.	book
2. running water		10.	race car
3. tree		11.	bicyclist climbing a hill
4. landslide		12.	screwdriver
5. hammer		13.	wheelbarrow
6. waterfall		14.	a cowboy roping a calf
7. rock		15.	a rolling marble
8. a pitcher winding up		16.	arrow

Energy of position is known as potential energy or stored energy. It is stored in an object as a result of a change in position. Therefore, the energy is at rest but has the potential for doing work.

B. Circle the numbers of the examples of potential energy in the list below.

1. jack-in-the-box		9.	a stretched slingshot
2. fast-moving river		10.	inflated balloon
3. wound-up propeller		11.	earthquake
4. mountain climber		12.	wind-blown flag
5. surfer riding a wave		13.	jumping porpoise
6. falling leaves		14.	falling brick
7. tank of gas		15.	landslide
8. bouncing ball		16.	rain storm

C. Underline the word in KINETIC that has to do with sports and recreation. Then list five activities related to the word that shows energy in motion.

The word is _____

1. _____ 4. _____

2. _____ 5. _____

3. _____

D. Underline the word in POTENTIAL that has to do with enjoying outdoors. Then list five items related to the word that offer examples of stored energy or energy at rest.

The word is _____

1. _____ 4. _____

2. _____ 5. _____

3. _____

Name _____ Date _____

54. Energy Crossword

Use the clues to complete the crossword puzzle. One term appears twice.

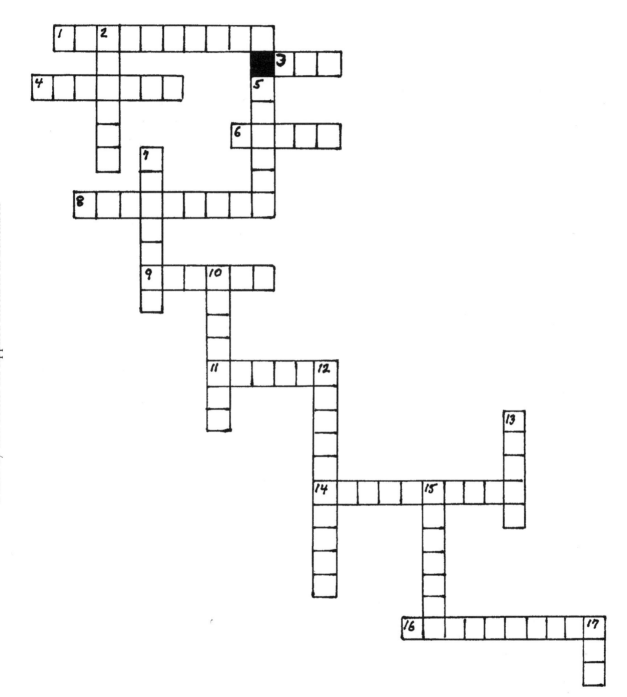

Energy Crossword
(con't)

Clues

Across

1. Form of energy.
3. An organ for receiving sound energy.
4. Energy produced by molecular motion.
6. Form of energy.
8. Energy at rest.
9. May be changed from one form to another.
11. Energy released through fission or fusion.
14. Heat energy transferred by the movement of liquids and gases.
16. A source of energy.

Down

2. Ability to do work.
5. Ch _ _ _ _ _ _ ; a source of energy.
7. Energy cannot be _ _ _ _ _ _ _ or destroyed.
10. Energy transmitted as heat waves.
12. Heat energy transferred through a substance by direct molecular contact.
13. Energy waves moving through the air.
15. A measure of heat energy.
18. The _ _ _ of conservation of energy.

55. Mixed-Up Energy

Unscramble each of the following sentences. Write the sentence in the appropriate space.

1. or is capacity Energy the ability to do work

_____

2. sun energy provides The solar

_____

3. Fuels chemical change energy are to burned heat into energy

_____

4. also stored energy resting Potential is as energy known or

_____

5. energy motion Kinetic of is energy

_____

6. nuclear energy atomic nucleus the Splitting produces

_____

7. produces nuclei The merging energy nuclear atomic more or two of

_____

8. changed from but may one another to be form destroyed Energy be cannot created or

_____

_____

9. exists forms different Energy in

_____

10. space Radiant through passes energy

_____

11. consumer amounts Large make to run energy machines of products

_____

12. fuels of source a are Fossil energy

_____

Name _____ Date _____

56. Sound Off

Sound is a form of energy produced by vibrating matter. Use the clues below to fill in the blanks.

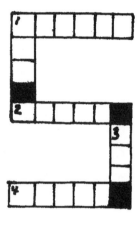
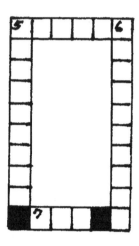
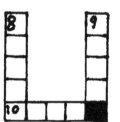

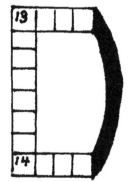

Sound Off
(con't)

Clues

Across

1. Reflecting sound waves from a surface.
2. Sound waves of irregular vibration in matter.
4. A pleasant pattern of sounds with reference to rhythm and tone.
5. A quantity of sound.
7. A musical note.
10. A stringed instrument.
13. Sound travels in these patterns.
14. The sound a broken twig makes.

Down

1. The organ of hearing.
3. Vibrations per second (abbr.).
5. This produces a quivering sound.
6. A tube that connects the middle ear with the pharynx.
8. A high or low sound.
9. Quality of musical sound.
11. Sound waves do not travel through this.
12. Material that carries sound waves.
13. To speak very low (plural).

57. The Human Ear

Locate and circle in the puzzle 15 terms related to the human ear and hearing. Write the name of each term next to its description. Terms may be up, down, forward, backward, and diagonal.

o	r	g	a	n	o	f	c	o	r	t	i	m
u	d	i	u	l	f	x	y	w	s	m	l	e
t	q	x	i	p	a	d	r	l	e	a	o	d
e	s	e	s	w	m	a	l	s	l	l	e	r
r	o	x	r	u	e	e	a	e	c	l	a	t
e	i	a	l	r	c	t	n	p	i	e	r	a
a	e	r	e	r	v	n	n	a	s	u	d	e
r	y	n	i	l	d	o	i	t	s	s	r	l
l	n	a	k	o	s	p	p	s	o	x	u	h
i	h	u	r	a	e	e	l	d	d	i	m	c
k	e	l	u	b	i	t	s	e	v	p	g	o
n	c	o	h	l	e	a	d	o	o	l	b	c

Description

1. The location for the sense organs for balance.
2. Contains the hearing receptors in the inner ear.
3. Directs sound waves to the eardrum.
4. Picks up and amplifies sound waves.
5. Receptors for sound.
6. Name for the outer ear.
7. Offers protection against foreign materials.
8. The collective name for three small bones.
9. The hammer (bone).
10. The anvil (bone).
11. The stirrup (bone).
12. Fills the inner ear.
13. An area of the inner ear.
14. Shaped like a snail; contains receptors of hearing.
15. Known as the tympanic membrane.

Term

1. _____
2. _____
3. _____
4. _____
5. _____
6. _____
7. _____
8. _____
9. _____
10. _____
11. _____
12. _____
13. _____
14. _____
15. _____

58. Matching Sounds

It isn't always easy to match a word representing a sound with a description of the sound. There are 25 "sound" words that need descriptions. Place the number of the description in the space to the left of the sound word.

Sound	Description
___ 1. yap	1. cannon noise
___ 2. alto	2. hoarse and rough
___ 3. snore	3. a low male voice
___ 4. pop	4. a sharp squeak
___ 5. roar	5. thunder is certainly this
___ 6. bleat	6. fireplace noise
___ 7. holler	7. a sharp outcry
___ 8. shriek	8. a high voice
___ 9. crackle	9. a sheep cry
___ 10. creak	10. a sharp, explosive sound
___ 11. loud	11. another word for shout
___ 12. bass	12. a puppy does this
___ 13. cry	13. a piercing, high pitch
___ 14. whine	14. a melodious rhythm
___ 15. whisper	15. cry of a horse
___ 16. chirp	16. expressive of merriment
___ 17. whistle	17. light rubbing, quick succession
___ 18. buzzing	18. a deep threatening sound
___ 19. howl	19. to sob
___ 20. growl	20. a bee in flight
___ 21. neigh	21. a mournful wail
___ 22. singing	22. a bird or cricket noise
___ 23. laugh	23. a sharp shrill
___ 24. rustle	24. low, breathing voice
___ 25. shrill	25. a tiresome expression

59. The Speed of Sound

A. It takes sound about five seconds to travel a mile. Sound travels 1100 feet per second. Fill in the empty blanks below to uncover the word that matches the description.

1.   T _ _ _ _ _   1. To move from one place to another.

2.   _ _ H _   2. Reflected sound.

3.   _ _ _ E _   3. A travel medium for sound.

4.   S _ _ _ _ _   4. Moving at a less than usual speed.

5.   _ P _ _ _   5. Rate of motion.

6.   _ _ _ E   6. A measurable period.

7.   _ E _ _ _ _ _   7. The quantity of something.

8.   D _ _ _ _ _ _ _   8. Separation in time.

9.   _ O _ _ _   9. Not liquid or gas.

10.   _ _ F _ _ _ _   10. To bend or throw back.

11.   S _ _ _ _ _ _   11. It takes 60 of these to make a minute.

12.   _ O _ _ _ _ _ _   12. Smallest amount; one or more atoms.

13.   _ _ U _ _   13. Energy of vibrating matter.

14.   _ _ _ N _ _   14. To rebound.

15.   _ _ _ _ _ D   15. Not a solid or gas.

B. Mystery Formula

The formula for calculating the speed of sound is as follows:

$$5 = \frac{8}{6}$$

What do the numbers in the formula mean? *Hint:* Look for clues in Part A.

C. Mystery Problem

If 8 equals 1980 feet and 6 equals 1.8 seconds, what is the distance sound traveled in feet per second?

D. Use these groups of answers from Part A in complete sentences:

1. 13, 10, 2

3. 9, 13, 15, 1

3. 5, 13, 6, 8

Name _____ Date _____

60. Very Sound Riddles and Problems

A. Here are six riddles to test the "riddle side" of your brain.

  1. What fruit has an ear but cannot hear?

  2. What animal is responsible for vibrations to occur?

  3. What animal needs 80 percent of the letters in sound to exist?

  4. What single object appears in a sound having a definite pitch?

  5. Why are housekeepers smarter than most scientists?

  6. What do you need to see before you can hear a dog whistle?

B. Here are six problems to challenge the "creative side" of your brain.

  1. Show using two words how a sound can pass through a solid.

  2. Show how sound waves might look under water.

  3. Show how to change sound to an echo.

  4. How many *sounds* can you get from the letters and numbers in the box?

s	u	t	2	14	o	s
a	s	c	o	s	e	u
8	n	o	6	u	n	h
s	d	s	m	7	r	d

  5. Show how to get an irritating sensation from PITCH.

  6. Show how an ear can be found in the chest region.

61. An "I" for an Eye

A. The eye is an organ of sight or vision. Light makes vision possible. There are 20 terms hidden in the puzzle that contain the letter "i". These terms relate in some way to light. Find and circle each term. Terms may be up, down, forward, backward and diagonal. Use the *Rhyming Word* column to help you locate the hidden terms.

m	i	c	r	o	s	c	o	p	e	j	v
o	t	a	w	o	b	n	i	a	r	n	i
l	e	n	e	p	i	m	a	g	e	o	s
n	p	i	g	k	r	p	w	v	f	i	i
o	o	t	a	o	u	i	r	x	r	t	o
i	c	e	r	p	v	e	s	l	a	c	n
t	s	r	i	o	n	h	a	m	c	e	a
o	i	l	m	c	i	c	o	s	t	l	t
m	r	e	i	n	o	g	i	b	i	f	h
a	e	t	e	f	u	r	e	a	o	e	g
f	p	w	i	t	i	s	i	v	n	r	i
o	m	b	d	i	o	r	o	h	c	x	s
l	e	n	s	h	z	n	i	a	r	b	y

B. Place the 20 terms in *alphabetical order.*

Terms

1. _____
2. _____
3. _____
4. _____
5. _____
6. _____
7. _____
8. _____
9. _____
10. _____
11. _____

Rhyming Word

1. local
2. crane
3. steroid
4. scrimmage
5. virus
6. kaleidoscope
7. garage
8. clearer
9. lotion
10. swerve (two words)
11. stethoscope

An "I" for an Eye
(con't)

12.	_____	12.	hypnotism
13.	_____	13.	duple (taken by twos)
14.	_____	14.	show
15.	_____	15.	inspection
16.	_____	16.	subtraction
17.	_____	17.	antenna
18.	_____	18.	brine
19.	_____	19.	flight
20.	_____	20.	decision

C. List *five* terms from Part B that are structures of the eye.

   1. _____   4. _____

   2. _____   5. _____

   3. _____

D. List *three* terms (beginning with the letter *r*) from Part B that relate in some way to the bending of light.

   1. _____

   2. _____

   3. _____

E. Write a statement describing how the terms listed below from Part B relate to vision.

   1. 17, 4, 2, and 10

_____

   2. 6 and 11

_____

Name _____ Date _____

62. Letters in a Box

Twelve terms related to light are scrambled in the boxes below. Unscramble each term and write it in the space under the box. Use the clues under the spaces to help you reveal the terms.

1.

_____

Source of light

2.

_____

Form of energy

3.

_____

How light travels (2 words)

4.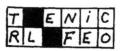

_____

Bouncing light

5.

_____

Light cannot pass through

6.

_____

Reflects light

7.

_____

Lens; thicker at edges than middle

8.

_____

Bending of light

9.

_____

Lens; thicker in middle than edges

10.

_____

Pattern of colors

11.

_____

Red, for example

12.

_____

Science of light

Name _____ Date _____

63. Let There Be Light

There are 24 items below related to light. Some may produce light, others may be affected or have an effect on light, and so on. Regardless, there will be a connection between the items and light. Use the two- or three-word clues to help you identify each item.

1. _____
   incandescent lamp

2. _____
   lens, retina, iris

3. _____
   sol, corona

4. _____
   insect larva

5. _____
   atmospheric discharge

6. _____
   colors, spectrum

7. _____
   flame, burning

8. _____
   unsteady flame, highway

9. _____
   wax, wick, birthday

10. _____
    self-luminous, night

11. _____
    flash, camera

12. _____
    burst forth, dynamite

13. _____
    front, car

14. _____
    intense beam

15. _____
    lens, mirror, planets

16. _____
    photoelectric, sun (2 words)

17. _____
    bouncing of light

18. _____
    minute objects, enlarged

19. _____
    chimney, log

20. _____
    bending of light

21. _____
    explosives, July 4th

22. _____
    small particle, burning

23. _____
    early, dawn

24. _____
    tubular, submarine

64. Light Statements

Unscramble the jumbled word in each statement and write it in the blank space.

1. Light _____ 186,000 miles per second.
   t e v l a r s

2. A _____ is an optical illusion.
   g r e m a i

3. The _____ controls the amount of light that enters the eye.
   i s i r

4. A black object does not _____ light.
   c f t e r l e

5. A prism _____ light into its colors.
   t r a s a e p s e

6. _____ is the branch of science which deals with the
   i t c o s p   nature and properties of light.

7. Light is _____ when it enters and when it leaves
   t c e d r a f r e   a lens.

8. The _____ of light depends on its frequency.
   l o c r o

9. A _____ is the number of waves that pass a
   y f n e e q u c r   given point in a given unit of time.

10. The layer of light-sensitive nerve endings lining the back of the

    eye is known as the _____.
    a t e n r i

11. Light is something that makes _____ possible.
    o i v n s i

12. Light seems to be made up of _____.
    l c s e t r i a p

13. Green plants use light to _____ their own food.
    d o p r e u c

Light Statements
(con't)

14. Sunlight is a _____ of light of all the different colors.
    n a i b n o i t o m c

15. Light can pass through _____ materials.
    n s p a a r t e r t n

16. _____ materials reflect all light.
    u p a e q o

17. Light is a form of energy made up of a stream of _____.
    o s p n h o t

18. Light travels in _____ lines.
    t a i s h g t r

19. Light takes about _____ minutes to travel from the sun to the earth.
    i t g e h

20. _____ materials transmit some light.
    r c u l s n a t t n e

65. Missing Letters

A. There are 32 words related to light listed below. Write the missing letter for each word in the space provided.

1. im__ge
2. energ__
3. __ransparent
4. concav__
5. p__oton
6. reti__a
7. l__ser
8. refrac__ion
9. c__nvex
10. sp__ctrum
11. ir__s
12. mir__or
13. sense or__an
14. __eflection
15. illu__inate
16. sig__t

17. particl__s
18. l__minous
19. opaqu__
20. wav__
21. __requency
22. c__lor
23. __peed
24. tra__sverse
25. __ologram
26. len__es
27. __olar
28. electrom__gnetic
29. tra__slucent
30. ampl__tude
31. chlorophy__l
32. __reen

B. Write the missing letters for each of the numbered items from Part A in the spaces provided.

1. Numbered Items: (3) __   (19) __   (25) __
2. Numbered Items: (2) __   (4) __   (17) __
3. Numbered Items: (27) __   (11) __
4. Numbered Items: (7) __
5. Numbered Items: (15) __   (1) __   (18) __   (29) __   (5) __
6. Numbered Items: (26) __   (6) __   (20) __   (10) __   (23) __
7. Numbered Items: (13) __   (28) __   (24) __   (9) __   (14) __
8. Numbered Items: (22) __   (12) __   (21) __
9. Numbered Items: (32) __   (30) __   (16) __   (8) __   (31) __

C. Now unscramble the letters of the numbered items in each group from Part B (except for number 4) to form a word. Use the words to complete the mystery statement.

Mystery Statement

__ __ __   __ __ __   __ __   __ __ __ __ __   __ __ __ __ __   __ __ __ __ __

__ __ __   __ __ __ __ __.

Name _____ Date _____

66. Cross Terms

Use the clues to help you find the missing words related to electricity or magnetism.

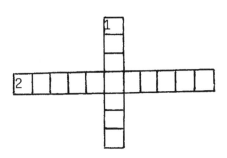 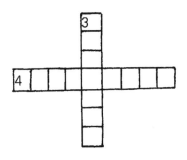

1. A magnet will do this to iron particles.
2. Electric energy currents

3. They carry a positive electrical charge.
4. They carry a negative electrical charge.

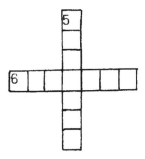 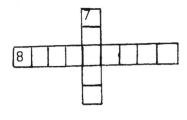

5. It has neither a positive nor a negative charge of electricity.
6. A single electric cell.

7. A force by which a magnet attracts certain objects.
8. Magnetic force around a magnet.

Cross Terms
(con't)

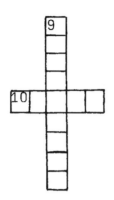

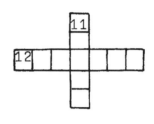

9. The force causing bodies to repel one another.

10. Regions in a magnetized body with high concentrations of magnetism.

11. A magnet cannot attract this writing material.

12. A device that has a magnetic needle turning freely on a pivot.

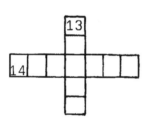

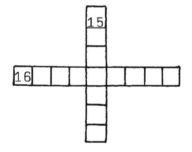

13. This habitable planet has a magnetic field.

14. Electricity in motion.

15. A soft, flexible material that cannot be picked up by a magnet.

16. Another name for magnetite.

Name _____ Date _____

67. Charged Up

A. Find and circle 20 words in the puzzle related to electric and magnetic forces. Then, in Part B, *alphabetize* them in the spaces below the puzzle. Words may be up, down, forward, backward, and diagonal.

```
b  h  t  u  o  s  y  x  a  e  m  e
u  e  l  e  p  e  r  n  v  p  i  l
l  o  y  x  l  f  e  i  y  r  d  e
b  p  m  o  o  h  t  n  e  o  f  c
e  y  p  r  t  i  t  e  v  g  t  t
g  k  c  l  s  y  a  u  i  n  c  r
r  e  o  o  x  m  b  t  t  o  a  o
a  v  p  r  p  q  y  r  a  t  r  n
h  f  i  e  l  d  s  a  g  o  t  x
c  u  r  r  e  n  t  l  e  r  t  i
x  e  a  k  o  s  x  y  n  p  a  e
y  h  t  r  o  n  e  u  t  r  o  n
```

B.

1. ◯ _ _ _ _ _

2. _ _ ◯ _ _ _

3. _ _ _ _ ◯ _

4. _ _ _ _ _

5. _ ◯ _ _ _ _

6. ◯ _ _ _ _ _

7. _ ◯ _ _ _ _ _ _

8. _ _ ◯ _ _

9. _ _ _ ◯ _

10. ◯ _ _ _

11. _ _ ◯ _ _ _ _ _

12. _ _ _ _ ◯ _ _

13. _ ◯ _ _ _ _

14. _ _ _ _ ◯

15. _ _ _ ◯ _

16. _ _ ◯ _ _ _ _

17. _ ◯ _ _ _

18. _ _ _ ◯ _

19. _ _ _ _ ◯

20. _ ◯ _ _

C. Place the numbered circled letters from Part B in the appropriate spaces below. If the words are alphabetized correctly, the statement will make sense.

__ __ k __ __ __ __ __ __ __ __   __ __ p __ __
7 10   15 9 19 1 17 11 18 16   12 8   13 7

__ __ __ __ __   t __ __ __ .
15 12 6 14 20   5 18 3

Name _____ Date _____

68. Mix and Match

A. A term related to electricity or magnetism appears backward within another word. Draw a line under the backward term, unscramble it, and write it in the space to the right. The first one is done for you.

1. env<u>elo</u>pe   pole
   _____

2. leper
   _____

3. wolfhound
   _____

4. crayon
   _____

5. odor
   _____

6. blubber
   _____

7. gulp
   _____

8. Ottawa
   _____

9. rabbit
   _____

10. Pliocene
    _____

B. List the unscrambled terms, 1 to 10, from Part A in the spaces to the right of the number. Place the letter of the matching description within the parenthesis next to the term. The first one is done for you.

1. ___pole____ (e)   a. a unit of electrical power

2. _____ ( )   b. lightning

3. _____ ( )   c. spiral turns of wire

4. _____ ( )   d. continuous transfer of energy

5. _____ ( )   e. region of a magnet

6. _____ ( )   f. electrical connection

7. _____ ( )   g. electric lamp

8. _____ ( )   h. push away

9. _____ ( )   i. move across a gap

10. _____ ( )   j. a type of magnet

Name _____ Date _____

69. All About Magnetism

Circle every other letter in the series of letters below. Then unscramble the letters to form a word associated with magnetism. Write the word in the space above the two clues.

1. e s a m t o b c l p i a y s

2. k e o t a n l m i a p g v e d i v t

3. a s c e t o d p r l

4. a p w l c e o e x r

5. e t m a o t v c l r k a z t

6. y n l o s i e r

7. b e q d u i c f n l

8. d o c o t s w h k r a e l h m s p e

9. t a e b y r k

10. l e d i v g k a o t w v p e r n

11. a p d s j i m e c v l i g t b o

12. m e g n w e f d o e r l

13. t f b e g o k r y c

14. o r t n v e w t b c a o k e x l

15. a m d o f a k t

16. e n t l r c o i v k s e

1. _____
   needle, direction

2. _____
   iron oxide

3. _____
   forces, end

4. _____
   like poles

5. _____
   unlike poles

6. _____
   Fe, element

7. _____
   area, forces

8. _____
   shape, magnet

9. _____
   rectangular, metal

10. _____
    minus charge

11. _____
    plus charge

12. _____
    magnetized, north

13. _____
    poles, between

14. _____
    atom, particle

15. _____
    element, smallest

16. _____
    attracts, magnet

70. Eight Mini-Problems

Here are eight mini-problems to keep your creative energy flowing:

1. Show how to write the word magnet to reveal a metal that is not attracted to a magnet.

2. A light bulb is sealed in one of the identical boxes below. Which box—A, B, or C—contains the bulb? How do you know?

A   B   C

15 pounds   6 pounds   7.5 pounds

3. Show a way to demonstrate a parallel circuit using only one word.

4. Show how like charges repel by using *one* + sign and *two* arrows.

5. An electrolyte is a liquid that conducts electricity. Salt water is an example of an electrolyte. Show, using a circle, the heaviest part of an electrolyte.

6. What does B and D represent in the diagram below?

C I R C U I T   circuit
A   B
C I R C U I T   circuit
C   D

7. An *amp* is a unit used to measure electric current. How many *amp's* can you spell from the letters in the box?

p	e	a	e	a
r	p	m	e	m
m	p	m	p	a
a	m	p	m	p
a	p	a	m	a

8. The unit of electrical energy is the kilowatt-hour. The electric utility company charges its customers for each kilowatt-hour of energy used. Think of a way to show what part of the kilowatt-hour should cost customers the least amount of money.

71. Solid Phase

Matter is anything that has weight and takes up space. Solid, a phase of matter, occupies a definite amount of space and has a definite shape. Use all the letters in each group below to spell the name of a solid object. Use the one-word clue to help you identify the solid.

1. B   U   R   E   R   B   Clue: bounce   Object: _____

2. L   P   A   I   C   S   T   Clue: synthetic   Object: _____

3. R   M   B   U   L   E   Clue: plant   Object: _____

4. P   R   E   A   P   Clue: wood   Object: _____

5. A   E   T   B   M   O   U
   O   I   L   Clue: vehicle   Object: _____

6. D   C   R   K   H   L   A
   O   A   B   Clue: write   Object: _____

7. R   I   N   H   C   L   E
   D   A   E   Clue: ceiling   Object: _____

8. R   A   G   T   I   U   Clue: strings   Object: _____

9. O   P   N   E   G   S   Clue: absorb   Object: _____

10. E   T   A   N   M   B   I
   R   O   U   Clue: drum   Object: _____

11. B   O   R   M   N   E   O   T   Clue: brass   Object: _____

12. R   O   G   E   T   U   S
   S   A   Clue: dinosaur   Object: _____

Name _____ Date _____

72. Liquid Phase

Matter is anything that has weight and takes up space. Liquid, a phase of matter, has a definite volume but takes the shape of the container that holds it. Use all the letters in each group below to spell the name of a liquid object. Use the one-word clue to help you identify the liquid.

1. L   W   A   F   T   R   E   L   A   Clue: stream   Object: _____

2. N   P   O   I   E   P   R
   A   T   T   C   I   I   Clue: rain   Object: _____

3. U   I   O   T   M   S   E   R   Clue: dampness   Object: _____

4. N   E   M   A   D   O   L   E   Clue: drink   Object: _____

5. K   A   E   R   E   B   R   Clue: shore   Object: _____

6. N   A   S   M   I   T   U   Clue: tidal   Object: _____

7. N   A   C   O   E   Clue: salt   Object: _____

8. E   G   L   A   N   I   S   O   Clue: flammable   Object: _____

9. S   E   A   M   T   Clue: vapor   Object: _____

10. S   Q   U   A   U   E   O   Clue: water   Object: _____

11. O   U   T   P   M   L   E   R   E   Clue: oil   Object: _____

12. N   O   I   T   A   R   I
   P   S   R   P   E   Clue: sweat   Object: _____

73. Gas Phase

Matter is anything that has weight and takes up space. Gas, a phase of matter, has no definite shape or volume and tends to occupy whatever space is available to it. Use all the letters in each group below to spell the name of a gaseous object or item. Use the one-word clue to help you identify the gas.

1. C E N I D R B
   O I X O A D   Clue: carbonated   Object: _____
                              (2 words)

2. N O Y X G E   Clue: life   Object: _____

3. N H G R E Y O D   Clue: lightest   Object: _____

4. M I E U L H   Clue: nonflammable Object: _____

5. E C I O L R H N   Clue: poisonous   Object: _____

6. E T M A N E H   Clue: marsh   Object: _____

7. E R O A N P P   Clue: barbecue   Object: _____

8. O A R N G   Clue: bulbs   Object: _____

9. B X E M R A D
   N O N O C O I   Clue: exhaust   Object: _____
                              (2 words)

10. O N N E   Clue: lamps   Object: _____

11. N U T E A B   Clue: petroleum   Object: _____

12. E N T E A H   Clue: C_2H_6 Object: _____

74. Mixed Matter

A. Find the examples of matter in each word below. Write the example next to the matching state or phase of matter. The first one is done for you.

1. Extinct	Solid	tin		
2. Terrain	Liquid	_____		
3. Thrice	Solid	_____	Solid	_____
4. Beverage	Solid	_____		
5. Reptile	Solid	_____		
6. Foreign	Solid	_____		
7. Argonaut	Gas	_____		
8. Impairment	Gas	_____		
9. Environment	Solid	_____		
10. Sediment	Solid	_____		
11. Janitor	Solid	_____		
12. Ecology	Solid	_____		
13. Neonatal	Gas	_____		
14. Chemist	Liquid	_____	Solid	_____
15. Improper	Solid	_____	Solid	_____
16. Automobile	Liquid	_____	Solid	_____
17. Calendar	Liquid	_____		
18. Aspirin	Solid	_____		
19. Turmoil	Liquid	_____		
20. Wrinkle	Solid	_____	Liquid	_____

B. Refer to Part A above to help you answer the following questions:

1. The answer to Item 18 is the name of an Egyptian snake. What letter added to the word would change the snake into a winged insect?

Mixed Matter
(con't)

2. What two things do the answers to Items 1 and 9 have in common?

3. How are the answers to Items 1 and 9 related to the answer to Item 6?

4. Add a different letter or two to the answer to Item 2 so you can complete each of the questions listed below:

   a. What organ did you discover?

   b. What do you call the seeds of cereal grass?

   c. What is the name for a line of railroad cars?

   d. What may result from a sudden twist of an ankle?

Name _____ Date _____

75. Puzzling Matter

Use the clues to help you fill in the spaces with terms related to MATTER.

Puzzling Matter
(con't)

Across

6. Color, shape, and hardness are examples.
7. Able to be hammered or rolled into thin sheets.
10. Chemical symbol, Number 8.
11. Another word for "stuff."
13. The action of a solid changing to a liquid state usually through the application of heat.
15. The area separating two objects.
17. Matter with unusual quality.
19. How tightly packed a substance's molecules are; the mass of a substance per unit volume.
22. Matter of definite chemical makeup.
23. A change in matter in which new substances with different properties are formed.
24. Matter being drawn out into wire: copper, for example.
26. Another word for state.
27. A gaseous mixture of highly ionized particles; referred to as the fourth state of matter.

Down

1. Matter passes from a solid to a gas without passing through a liquid phase.
2. A common example of a liquid.
3. A state of matter.
4. Not a solid or liquid.
5. A measure of gravity.
8. The science of matter.
9. The amount of space an object takes up.
12. A transparent solid; you can see through it.
14. A measure of the amount of matter contained in an object.
16. This causes water to turn into ice.
18. Rubber has this special stretching quality.
20. A change in matter which does not change the individual molecules.
21. A tiny amount of matter.
25. To shift from one form to another.

76. Boxed In

There are 12 terms related to atomic structures trapped in the boxes below. In order to free each one, circle the letters that spell the name of the item. Use the one-word hint to help you.

1.
A	O	E	S
I	U	R	L
U	N	M	C

Hint: center

2.
E	R	E	O
S	N	O	R
T	L	C	P

Hint: negative

3.
N	E	L
R	A	O
U	T	P

Hint: neutron

4.
N	N	O	E
C	E	P	S
T	R	L	U

Hint: uncharged

5.
O	N	S	R
E	C	U	E
P	T	L	O

Hint: positive

6.
N	U	B
E	S	O
R	A	M

Hint: atomic

7.
L	M	A	S
S	M	T	B
Y	S	E	O

Hint: shorthand

8.
I	E	O
T	O	L
P	R	N

Hint: charged

9.
L	C	L
O	E	R
E	T	V

Hint: energy

10.
N	E	A	H
U	T	M	I
R	O	T	O

Hint: smallest

11.
M	G	S
R	A	V
T	I	S

Hint: weight

12.
P	C	O	R
I	S	P	T
I	E	D	N

Hint: table

Use the answers from the boxes above to fill in the empty spaces.

13. An _____ is an electrically charged atom.

14. Cl is the chemical _____ for chlorine.

15. The nucleus of an atom contains neutrons and _____.

16. An atom is electrically _____.

77. Elements Everywhere

Use the clues to find each of the elements listed below:

Element   Clues

1.   __ E __ __ __   1.   An inert gas

2.   L __ __ __   2.   Latin name: plumbum

3.   __ __ __ __ E __ __ __ __ __   3.   Named after Albert

4.   __ __ __ M __ __ __   4.   Has 48 protons and 48 electrons

5.   __ E __ __ __   5.   Atomic mass = 140.12

6.   __ __ N __   6.   Rhymes with blink

7.   __ __ T __ __ __ __ __   7.   Sounds like alimony

8.   __ S __ __ __ __ __ __   8.   Has 85 protons

9.   __ E __ __   9.   An inert gas

10.   __ __ __ V __ __   10.   Lone Ranger's horse

11.   __ __ __ E __ __ __ __   11.   Neutron number = 44.96

12.   __ __ R __ __ __   12.   Black, Number 6

13.   __ __ Y __ __ __   13.   Atomic mass = 16

14.   __ __ W __ __ __ __ __ __ __ 14.   Look for Lr

15.   __ __ __ H __ __ __   15.   Neutron number = 3.946

16.   __ __ __ __ E __   16.   Neutron number = 30.69

17.   __ __ R __ __ __   17.   Has 96 electrons

18.   __ __ __ __ E __   18.   One cent

Name _____ Date _____

78. Say What?

A word in each sentence below needs to be replaced by a correct word before the sentence makes sense. Draw a line through the incorrect word and write the correct word above the line. The first one is done for you.

1. Matter is made up of very small particles called atoms.

2. Pringle atoms of any element are too small to be seen.

3. An atom is the tallest particle of an element.

4. Atoms are the basic building stocks of matter.

5. The gluteus is the center of an atom.

6. An atom is considered to be electrically normal.

7. Newtons and protons are found in the nucleus of an atom.

8. A neutron has no barge.

9. An electron unravels around the nucleus of an atom.

10. Electrons are believed to move at a rabid pace.

11. Electrons move in definite regions called electron crowds or energy levels.

12. The pass number indicates the total number of protons and neutrons found in the nucleus of an atom.

13. Protons and neutrons are thought to be made of smaller particles called quartz.

14. The atomic number tells how many croutons are in the nucleus.

15. A sodium atom has 11 protons. It also has 11 rejectons.

16. Some chemical symbols come from the satin name of the element.

17. Each comical symbol consists of one or two letters.

18. The chemical thimble for chlorine is Cl.

19. Ag is the chemical symbol for sliver.

20. An isopod is an atom whose nucleus contains the same number of protons but different numbers of neutrons.

Name _____ Date _____

79. Chemical Symbol Parade

Find the chemical symbols for the elements listed in each group below. Write the symbol in the space under each element. Then put the symbols together to spell the name of the mystery word. Use the clues and a periodic table to help you.

1. Arsenic   Phosphorus   Chlorine

   _____   _____   _____

2. Thorium   Protactinium

   _____   _____

3. Cerium   Radium

   _____   _____

4. Nitrogen   Cobalt   Radium   Oxygen

   _____   _____   _____   _____

5. Dysprosium   Boron   Oxygen

   _____   _____   _____

   Nitrogen   Oxygen

   _____   _____

6. Lanthanum   Cerium   Nitrogen

   _____   _____   _____

7. Oxygen   Carbon   Boron   Radium

   _____   _____   _____   _____

8. Barium   Rhodium   Rubidium   Uranium

   _____   _____   _____   _____

9. Erbium   Oxygen   Rhodium

   _____   _____   _____

   Osmium   Carbon   Indium

   _____   _____   _____

10. Argon   Nitrogen   Lutetium

   _____   _____   _____

11. Nitrogen   Bromine   Oxygen   Cobalt

   _____   _____   _____   _____

12. Erbium   Polonium   Potassium

   _____   _____   _____

1. A hook for holding objects together. _____

2. A route or course.

   _____

3. Horses in a contest.

   _____

4. Small, gray animal with a bushy ringed tail. _____

5. Not anybody. _____

6. A knight's weapon.

   _____

7. A hooded poisonous snake.

   _____

8. Broad green-leaf plants with thick, juicy, pink stems. _____

9. Large plant-eating African mammal. _____

10. Relating to the moon.

   _____

11. A partly broken range horse.

   _____

12. A card game. _____

Name _____ Date _____

Chemical Symbol Parade
(con't)

13. Boron   Chromium   Iodine

    _____   _____   _____

14. Hydrogen   Argon   Nitrogen

    _____   _____   _____

     Aluminum   Tungsten

    _____   _____

15. Sulfur   Phosphorus   Nitrogen

    _____   _____   _____

     Oxygen   Erbium

    _____   _____

16. Iridium   Phosphorus   Tantalum

    _____   _____   _____

17. Ruthenium   Sulfur   Tungsten

    _____   _____   _____

     Aluminum

    _____

18. Calcium   Indium   Boron

    _____   _____   _____

19. Sodium   Titanium   Rhenium

    _____   _____   _____

20. Titanium   Carbon   Actinium

    _____   _____   _____

13. A baby's bed. _____

14. A large sea animal related to the dolphin. _____

15. An individual. _____

16. A nocturnal hoofed mammal with a long flexible snout.

    _____

17. Large northern sea mammal.

    _____

18. A private room on a ship.

    _____

19. Sensory membrane of the eye.

    _____

20. More than one flowering plant of the desert.

    _____

Name _____ Date _____

80. Where Are They?

Let's go on a treasure hunt. Answer the following items carefully examining the Periodic Table of Elements.

1. Find an element with a *female bird* as part of its name.

2. Find *two* elements that have the same insect's name in them.

3. What *four* elements have the word *tin* as part of their names?

4. In what element's name will you find an elarged growth of a plant tissue?

5. Three-fourths of this element's name is made up of a term which describes one billion years of geologic time. What is it?

6. What element has a word in its name that refers to something from a past era?

7. Find a word in an element's name that describes what happens to skin from overexposure to the sun.

8. What element holds the Spanish word for gold (oro)?

9. Find an element that has "all" in the middle.

10. The chemical symbol for silver is Ag. What other element has "ag" as part of its name?

11. If you remove the letters *t, a,* and *i* from the name of a certain element, you'll have the name of a nocturnal pouched animal. What is the element?

12. Find *two* elements that have three *i*'s in each of their names.

13. In what element can you find *flu* spelled backwards?

14. Webster's New Encyclopedic Dictionary describes a brown singing bird with short rounded wings and a short erect tail. Its name rhymes with chin. In what element is the name of this bird hiding?

15. What element has a number spelled backwards in the middle of its name?

Name _____ Date _____

81. Chemistry Terms, Part 1

There are 15 chemistry terms in the box below. Find and shade in the letters of the 15 terms that match their descriptions. Write the terms in the spaces to the left of their descriptions. Terms may appear across and down in the box. Unscramble the unshaded letters to reveal the answer to the mystery item.

S	U	B	S	T	A	N	C	E	M
C	O	M	P	O	U	N	D	P	O
G	A	S	S	O	L	I	D	A	L
C	B	O	N	D	I	O	N	R	E
R	O	X	I	D	E	I	R	T	C
Y	T	A	T	O	M	L	E	I	U
S	G	M	A	T	T	E	R	C	L
T	I	L	I	Q	U	I	D	L	E
A	M	I	X	T	U	R	E	E	S
L	F	N	E	L	E	M	E	N	T

Terms

1. _____
2. _____
3. _____
4. _____
5. _____
6. _____
7. _____
8. _____
9. _____
10. _____
11. _____
12. _____
13. _____
14. _____
15. _____

Descriptions

1. Smallest particle.
2. Hydrogen's state of matter (lightest).
3. Carbon is one; so is argon.
4. A charged particle.
5. Faucet water; state of matter.
6. Na + Cl = Sodium Chloride. Sodium Chloride, salt, is an example.
7. The smallest part of a compound that has all the properties of the compound (plural).
8. An attractive force between groups of atoms.
9. Has weight and takes up space.
10. The smallest part or fragment of an atom.
11. An iron magnet's state of matter.
12. Two or more substances that have been combined, but not chemically changed.
13. A compound of oxygen with an element.
14. Physical matter from which something is made.
15. Diamonds, rubies, garnets, and emeralds are found in this form.

Mystery Item

How can a mixture be separated? Well, one way is by __ __ __ __ __ __ __ __ __ __ the mixture.

82. Chemistry Terms, Part 2

There are 15 chemistry terms in the box below. Find and shade in the letters of the 15 terms that match their descriptions. Write the terms in the spaces to the left of their descriptions. Terms may appear across and down in the box. Unscramble the unshaded letters to reveal the answer to the mystery item.

R	S	U	B	S	C	R	I	P	T
E	S	O	L	U	T	I	O	N	C
A	D	I	A	T	O	M	I	C	A
C	M	V	U	B	A	S	E	L	T
T	O	E	S	O	L	U	T	E	A
A	L	C	A	L	L	O	Y	R	L
N	E	R	A	D	I	C	A	L	Y
T	A	C	I	D	S	A	L	T	S
N	S	O	L	V	E	N	T	O	T
I	M	I	S	C	I	B	L	E	C
T	S	M	T	O	X	I	C	L	A

Terms

1. _____
2. _____
3. _____
4. _____
5. _____
6. _____
7. _____
8. _____
9. _____
10. _____
11. _____
12. _____
13. _____
14. _____
15. _____

Descriptions

1. The liquid in which a solute dissolves.
2. The gram-molecular weight of a molecular substance.
3. Poisonous
4. A substance which acquires protons from another substance. Ex: lye.
5. An element or compound entering into a chemical action.
6. A liquid containing a dissolved substance.
7. A material composed of two or more metals.
8. A group of atoms that acts as if it were a single atom.
9. Two atoms
10. A number written below and to the side of a chemical symbol.
11. A substance that speeds a chemical reaction without itself being changed.
12. The substance that dissolves in another substance.
13. Sodium chloride, for example.
14. A substance in solution which yields hydrogen ions.
15. Capable of being mixed.

Mystery Item

_ _ _ _ _ _ _ _   _ _ _ _ _ _ _ of elements in the Periodic Table are called groups. A horizontal row of elements in the Periodic Table is known as a period.

83. Twist and Turn

A mixture occurs when two or more substances are put together so that their separate properties are unchanged. In other words, the different materials have not been chemically united. Each substance can be in various amounts and easily separated. For example, it wouldn't be difficult to remove sand from water.

Identify the substances that are mixed together in the boxes below. They may appear as chemical symbols or words broken down into two or three letter groups. Write the name of each substance in the spaces under the box. The first one is done for you.

1.

sa	su	nd
sug	ar	nd
gar	sa	sug
nd	ar	gar
su		

sugar
_____

sand
_____

2.

on	Fe	ir	S
sul	ir	fur	
Fe	on	S	Fe

_____

_____

3.

gr	sti	av	cks
sti	gr	el	av
el	cks	gr	el

_____

_____

4.

pe	pe	ce	
as	ri	as	ce
pe	as	ri	

_____

_____

5.

rr	let	ots	ets
ce	rr	be	tu
ca	ce	be	

_____

_____

6.

Cu	le	Fe	Pb
co	ad	pp	Fe
er	on	ir	

_____

_____

Twist and Turn
(con't)

7.

sa	lt	pp	
pe	pep		
sa	er	lt	er
per			

_____

_____

8.

app	or	pl	ora
es	ng	an	ges
ap	les	es	

_____

_____

9.

mes	di	Ni	es
Ni	dim	Ni	Ni

_____

_____

10.

su	sa	sug	lt
ar	lt	gar	su
		sug	

_____

_____

A Challenge

What do you think the box of letters below represents?

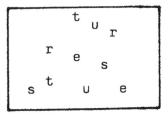

Name _____ Date _____

84. Compounds

Compounds are materials made of two or more kinds of atoms held together in chemical combinations. Water, H_2O, is an example.

A. Use a Periodic Table of Elements to find the chemical symbols that match the atomic numbers listed below. Write the symbols in the spaces provided. In every instance, a symbol will be repeated in the chemical formula. Finally, write the chemical formula for each compound *above* the name of the compound. The first one is done for you.

Atomic Numbers	Chemical Symbols	Chemical Formulas
1. 25	Mn	MnO_2
8 8	O O	manganese dioxide
2. 14	_____	_____
8 8	_____ _____	silicon dioxide
3. 6	_____	_____
8 8	_____ _____	carbon dioxide
4. 11 17	_____ _____	_____
		sodium chloride
5. 6	_____	_____
1 1 1 1	__ __ __ __	methane
6. 6 6 6	__ __ __	
1 1 1 1	__ __ __ __	_____
1 1 1 1	__ __ __ __	propane
7. 29 16	_____ _____	_____
8 8 8 8	__ __ __ __	copper sulfate
8. 20 6	_____ _____	_____
8 8 8	__ __ __	calcium carbonate

Compounds
(con't)

9.	1	1	_____	_____	_____
					hydrogen peroxide
	8	8	_____	_____	
10.	26	26	_____	_____	_____
					iron (III) oxide
	8 8 8		___ ___ ___		

B. The compounds in Part A represent the three states of matter: solid, liquid, and gas. Three of the solid compounds have an oxide containing two atoms of oxygen. What are they? They are:

1. _____

2. _____

3. _____

C. *A Make-Believe Compound*

If the make-believe elements listed below combined in alphabetical order, what would be the result?

Us + G + Bo

The result would be a _____ compound.

85. Chemistry Mini-Problems

Push the creative-thinking button and sharpen your problem-solving skills at the same time. Here are eight mini-challenges for you to tackle.

1. Think of a way to produce iron (Fe) from the numbers 77, 8 and 7.

2. What does the illustration represent?

1 cents

Chemical   5 cents

10 cents

25 cents

3. What does the illustration represent?

        M
P   H   A   S   E
        T
        T
        E
        R

4. Find a prisoner, an animal, a star, and a charged particle in the term CONCENTRATED SOLUTION.

5. Think of a way to make OXYGEN from two HYDROGENs shown below.

H Y   D Y H
   D R   R
      O   G
   N E G   O G E N

6. Three siblings live in the same house. They are Nathaniel, Nadine, and Natalie. How might a chemist refer to these children?

7. Use only two words to describe how soft water can be turned into hard water.

8. How can you reduce the weight of a 125-pound male sheep to 1/1000 kilogram?

86. All About Heat

Heat may be defined as a form of moving energy. The energy moves from anything having a higher temperature to anything having a lower temperature. Heat, then, is a measure of the total energy of motion of all the molecules in an object.

Use the clues to find terms related to heat.

Clues

1.   H __ __ __ __ __   1.   A device that produces heat.

2.   __ __ E __ __ __   2.   Heat is a form of this.

3.   __ A __ __ __ __ __   3.   A unit used to measure heat.

4.   __ __ __ __ T __ __   4.   Heat energy in motion.

5.   __ H __ __ __ __ __   5.   A rising body of warm air.

6.   __ E __ __   6.   -273°C; absolute _____.

7.   __ __ __ __ A __ __ __   7.   Heat wave energy.

8.   __ __ __ T __ __ __ __   8.   A tiny fragment of heated material.

a

n

d

9.   M __ __ __ __   9.   Butter does this when it warms.

10.   __ O __ __ __ __ __ __ __ 10.   Heat transmits readily through this.

11.   __ __ __ __ __ R __ __ __ __ __ 11.   A measure of how hot or cold something is.

12.   __ __ __ __ E __ __ __ __   12.   Rising hot air.

13. __ __ __ __ __ __ H __ __ __   13.   A temperature scale.

14.   __ __ __ __ __ E   14.   A source of birthday heat.

15.   __ __ __ __ __ A __ __ __   15.   Poor conductor of heat.

16.   __ __ __ __ T __ __ __   16.   A producer of heat.

87. Every Other Letter

A. A conductor is a substance that conducts or transfers heat readily. A solid material, like metal, makes a good conductor. The molecules in a solid are packed together.

There are seven conductors listed below. Fill in the empty spaces with the missing letters. Use the scrambled clue word as a key to the answer.

			Clue Word	
1.	C	_ o _ p _ r	1.	c p p o r e
2.	O	o _ e	2.	o e r
3.	N	_ i _ k _ l	3.	k l i e c n
4.	D	d _ n _ m _ t _	4.	m y i e d t n a
	*U			
5.	C	_ h _ o _ i _ m	5.	m o m c r u h i
6.	T	t _ n	6.	i t n
7.	S	_ i _ v _ r	7.	l v i r s e

B. A radiator releases heat by transferring energy in waves through space. There are seven items listed below known to radiate heat or allow for radiation to occur. Fill in the empty spaces with the missing letters. Use the scrambled clue word as a key to the answer.

			Clue Word	
1.	R	r _ d _ a _ o _	1.	a t a i d r o r
2.	A	_ t _ o _ p _ e _ e	2.	h m p e t a s o r e
3.	D	d _ n _ i _ g	3.	n i d a g c n
4.	I	_ n _ r _ r _ d (heater)	4.	f e d i n r a r
	*A			
5.	T	t _ e _ m _ l	5.	r t l e h a m
6.	E	_ x _ r _ i _ e	6.	e e s r i x c e
7.	S	s _ n _ h _ n _	7.	u s n i h n e s

C. Take the starred letters in Parts A and B, make one letter lower case, and produce an example of an object that conducts heat.

© 1995 by The Center for Applied Research in Education

88. It's in the Term

Read each statement carefully. Then answer the items related to the term.

1. The movement of cold and warm water molecules creates CONVECTION CURRENTS. Wind and ocean currents are examples of convection currents.
   a. Find a mongrel dog in CURRENTS.
   b. Find "money paid for the use of property" in CURRENTS.

2. RADIATION is the flow of energy in the form of traveling rays. Infrared heat rays are good examples.
   a. Find the Spanish word for day in RADIATION.
   b. Find the Spanish word for uncle in RADIATION.

3. TEMPERATURE is a measure of an object to transfer heat to or absorb heat from other objects. In other words, it is a measure of how hot or cold something is.
   a. Find a word that means "a process of painting" in TEMPERATURE.
   b. Find one of the five major divisions of geologic time in TEMPERATURE.

4. COMBUSTION, the process of burning, releases heat and light.
   a. Find a fleshy crest on the head of a chicken in COMBUSTION.
   b. Find a vehicle for carrying passengers in COMBUSTION.
   c. Find a word that means "complete failure" in COMBUSTION.

5. A THERMAL may be described as a rising body of warm air.
   a. Find a male animal in THERMAL.
   b. Find something "bad" in THERMAL.

6. The BOILING POINT refers to the temperature at which water changes to steam.
   a. Find something "greasy" in BOILING POINT.
   b. Find a Hawaiian food made from the taro root in BOILING POINT.

7. ENDOTHERMIC refers to the absorption of heat.
   a. Find a prefix meaning "in" in ENDOTHERMIC.
   b. Find a "speck" in ENDOTHERMIC.
   c. Find a word meaning "additional one" in ENDOTHERMIC.
   d. Find a word meaning "to carry out" in ENDOTHERMIC.

8. ERUPT can refer to a sudden release of heat. A volcano may erupt with a violent explosion, for example.
   a. Find a word meaning "being ahead of an opponent" in ERUPT.
   b. Find a word from right to left meaning "free from something" in ERUPT.

89. Seven-Letter Puzzle

A. Terms related to heat are scattered about the puzzle. There are several terms that are not related to heat. Twenty-four words from the list below can be found in the puzzle. As you find a word, shade in the spaces containing the letters. The darkened spaces will reveal the seven letters necessary to form the word that answers the Bonus Item, Part C. As a challenge, you will have to unscramble the letters to find the word. Terms may be up, down, forward, backward and diagonal.

M	E	A	S	U	R	E	O	C	O	L	D	T	A	L	C	R
O	X	Y	G	E	N	M	E	A	I	P	M	U	S	P	Y	G
W	A	K	C	S	W	O	U	L	R	C	J	I	S	O	L	D
A	H	Z	O	M	D	L	N	O	L	D	B	X	O	S	O	E
T	C	I	L	O	L	E	B	R	S	A	L	T	L	A	T	E
E	F	C	T	K	O	C	D	I	C	A	G	W	I	T	R	P
R	P	L	V	E	G	U	G	E	X	I	T	Q	D	U	U	S
I	O	D	I	N	E	L	B	A	R	I	U	M	A	R	S	B
M	O	R	S	E	T	E	N	E	R	G	Y	C	I	N	A	A
O	L	C	E	L	E	M	E	N	T	C	V	L	A	B	E	S
T	E	N	O	M	I	O	Q	D	N	N	S	T	E	A	M	E
I	O	N	S	R	U	M	L	I	H	O	C	H	S	V	B	F
O	A	W	O	V	K	A	Z	P	M	R	A	T	O	M	A	S
N	P	N	D	T	O	L	T	A	H	O	L	I	R	G	Y	Z
C	U	R	I	U	M	A	I	R	E	B	E	J	E	C	T	Y

motion	tone	flask	cold	eject
Alamo	smoke	solid	melt	calorie
sold	steam	speed	freeze	Morse
old	white	elm	exit	electricity
water	scale	Monet	energy	molecule
elastic	late	air	rapid	thermal

Seven-Letter Puzzle
(con't)

B. Some of the answers from the seven-letter puzzle will match the items below. Hunt them down and place the answers in the spaces to the right of the descriptions.

1. A code; dots and dashes.   _____

2. A famous artist.   _____

3. To throw out or evict.   _____

4. Remember the __ __ __ __ __.   _____

5. A way out; an egress.   _____

C. Bonus Item
    This kind of energy releases tremendous amounts of heat.

    It is known as __ __ __ __ __ __ __ energy.

90. Middle-Letter Message

The middle letters from top to bottom in the puzzle form the words necessary to complete the message below. Fill in the empty spaces with the missing letters. Use the clues to help you find the missing letters in the puzzle.

	Clues
1. _ _ _ _ _ _	1. Quick to act
2. _ _ _ _ _ _	2. To seek rest
3. _ _ _ _ _ _	3. Upright
4. _ _ _ _ _ _	4. Slender American snake
5. _ _ _ _ _ _	5. Universal liquid
6. _ _ _ _ _ _	6. Exceeds in size
7. _ _ _ _ _ _	7. A calm or peace
8. _ _ _ _ _ _ _ _	8. Distinctive; high quality
9. _ _ _ _ _ _	9. To form letters
10. _ _ _ _ _ _ _ _	10. Glazed, salted cracker
11. _ _ _ _ _ _	11. Made into yarn and thread
12. _ _ _ _ _ _ _	12. A pugilist, for example
13. _ _ _ _ _ _	13. Preferred style
14. _ _ _ _ _ _	14. A strong desire
15. _ _ _ _ _ _	15. An inn for motorists
16. _ _ _ _ _ _	16. Used to enrich soil
17. _ _ _ _ _ _	17. Facial expression of pleasure
18. _ _ _ _ _ _	18. Not real; counterfeit
19. _ _ _ _ _ _ _ _	19. A North American wild sheep
20. _ _ _ _ _ _	20. To toss a baseball to a batter

_ _ _ _ _ _ _ _ _ _ _ _ _ becomes useful when it is converted into

_ _ _ _ and _ _ _ _ _ _.

91. Keen Machines

A. A machine may be any device that changes the direction or size of a force. If you use a jack handle to lift a car when removing a tire, you are changing the direction and the size of the force. Therefore, the jack handle would be an example of a machine.

Circle the example of a machine or part of a machine in each of the series of words below.

1. ball sand lathe crust plaza	(Letter 3)
2. meteor orange shovel lamp sky	(Letter 2)
3. ground vest map axle tuatara	(Letter 4)
4. scissors velour saffron cement rock	(Letter 5)
5. baste mutt tapir shoe horn rust	(Letter 4)
6. weight wheelbarrow brick rubber steel	(Letter 7)
7. shrew screw ball bolder strata	(Letter 3)
8. ledge edge wedge ridge caldera	(Letter 2)
9. steer gear glass magma trench	(Letter 3)
10. statue bicycle string clay paint	(Letter 1)
11. tongs friction rayon ore luster	(Letter 2)
12. ball silicon humus nutcracker putty	(Letter 2)
13. wallet tractor parka moa escrow	(Letter 5)
14. ice granite shirt quartz broom	(Letter 5)
15. snake rock rake turnip nail	(Letter 2)
16. crowbar butte rubber crystal atom	(Letter 1)
17. coin fort cirrus hammer iron	(Letter 1)
18. paste dough concrete winch nimbus	(Letter 2)
19. syncline anticline incline rug bottle	(Letter 6)
20. pulley marble dam rope spicule	(Letter 5)
21. cumulus pipe piston brick speed	(Letter 3)

B. There are 21 letters in the mystery four-word statement. Use the letters from the answers indicated in parenthesis, 1 through 21, to help you solve the mystery.

_ _ _ _ _   _ _ _   _ _ _ _ _   _ _ _ _ _ _ _ _.

92. Two Missing Letters

A. Read each of the statements below. Write the missing letters of the key word in the empty spaces.

1. Force may be considered exerted __ __ rength; a push or pull.

2. Movement is another word for __ __ tion.

3. __ __ wton discovered the Laws of Motion.

4. Acceleration means __ __ ange in motion.

5. The attractive force between masses is known as __ __ avity.

6. __ __ ight is a measure of the force of attraction on the mass of an object.

7. Newton's First Law of Motion states that an object will remain at rest or move at a constant speed in a straight line unless it is acted on by an __ __ balanced force.

8. Newton's Second Law of Motion states that the unbalanced force acting on an object is equal to the mass of the object times its __ __ celeration.

9. Newton's Third Law of Motion states that for every action there is an equal and opposite __ __ action.

10. Speed may be considered the rate of change in __ __ sition.

11. __ __ locity is the rate of motion in a certain direction.

12. If acceleration refers to change in speed, then a car that slows down is accelerating and __ __ celerating.

13. __ __ iction is an example of an unbalanced force.

14. __ __ ertia is the tendency of an object to remain at rest or in motion. The object resists any change.

15. __ __ rces always act in pairs. If you press your hand against a wall, the wall exerts an equal force against your hand.

Two Missing Letters
(con't)

B. The numbered statements from Part A appear in parentheses below. Write the answers to each statement next to the number. The combined answers will reveal a word that matches a description. Write the letter of the matching description in the space provided. The first one is done for you.

Description

_d_	1.	gr	(5)	+	in	(14)	= grin	a.	Opposite of less
__	2.		(4)	+		(14)	=	b.	A skin disorder
__	3.		(10)	+		(1)	=	c.	Found below the lower lip
__	4.		(2)	+		(11)	=	d.	A type of smile
__	5.		(10)	+		(9)	=	e.	Largest quantity
__	6.		(1)	+		(7)	=	f.	Area or section of land
__	7.		(2)	+		(9)	=	g.	Fixed timber in an upright position
__	8.		(2)	+		(1)	=	h.	A tiny opening
__	9.		(8)	+		(3)	=	i.	To knock senseless
__	10.		(8)	+		(9)	=	j.	To set in motion

93. Pyramid Power

The nine pyramids contain letters needed to spell the answers to the 12 items below. Some pyramids have enough letters to produce two answers; one pyramid offers no help at all. Write the letters in the empty spaces and the number of the pyramid in parentheses to indicate where the letters came from.

1.
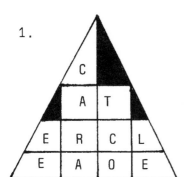

2.
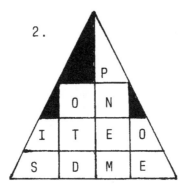

3.
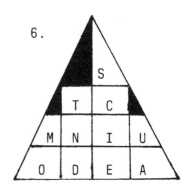

4.
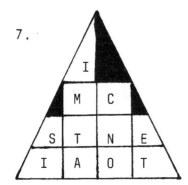

5.
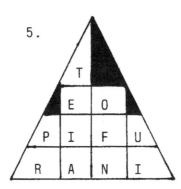

6.
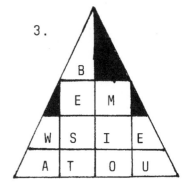

7.
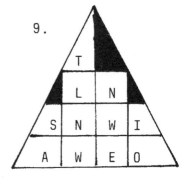

8.
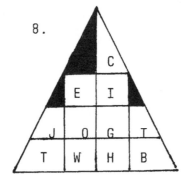

9.
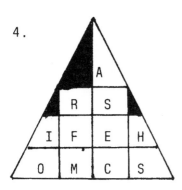

© 1995 by The Center for Applied Research in Education

Name _____ Date _____

Pyramid Power
(con't)

1. A push or pull.   _ _ _ _ _ _   (   )

2. Property of matter
   which resists change   _ _ _ _ _ _ _ _   (   )
   in motion.

3. A measure of the amount
   of matter.   _ _ _ _   (   )

4. To change from one
   place to another.   _ _ _ _ _ _   (   )

5. Rate of motion.   _ _ _ _ _   (   )

6. Offered explanations
   for force and motion.   _ _ _ _ _ _   (   )

7. He came up with three
   of these.   _ _ _ _   (   )

8. To change in motion.   _ _ _ _ _ _ _ _ _ _   (   )

9. The measure of mass.   _ _ _ _ _ _   (   )

10. Separation in time
    and space.   _ _ _ _ _ _ _ _   (   )

11. One object exerts a
    force on a second object.   _ _ _ _ _ _   (   )

12. The measured action
    of an activity.   _ _ _ _   (   )

94. Vowel Trouble

A. There are 20 terms below related to force and motion. Unfortunately, the vowel letters—a, e, i, o, and u—are missing. Use the missing vowel letters to fill in the empty spaces.

1. __ n __ r t __ __

2. a c c __ l __ r __ t __

3. v __ l __ c __ t y

4. f r __ c t __ __ n

5. r __ __ c t __ __ n

6. g r __ v __ t y

7. __ m p __ t __ s

8. m __ s s

9. __ n __ r g __

10. d __ c __ l __ r __ t __

11. __ n b __ l __ n c __ d

12. __ c t __ __ n

13. d __ s t __ n c __

14. w __ __ g h t

15. c __ n t r __ f u g __ l

16. N __ w t __ n

17. d __ r __ c t __ __ n

18. b __ l __ n c __ d

19. s p __ __ d

20. m __ m __ n t __ m

B. Match the numbers of eight terms from Part A with the following one-word clues. Place the number in the space to the right of the term.

1. rub   ___

2. laws   ___

3. density   ___

4. backward   ___

5. attraction   ___

6. slowing   ___

7. equilibrium   ___

8. response   ___

Note: If you total the numbers for the eight one-word examples, you should get 84.

Name _____ Date _____

95. A Mix of Riddles and Problems

Wake up the riddle/problem center of your brain and see how many of the following items you can master.

1. What state in the United States holds the largest quantity of matter?

2. Mrs. Entum had six children—4 boys and 2 girls. What might you call her if you didn't know her first name?

3. How can you get the word "woo" out of weight?

4. What do these letters represent?

   E Q F U O I L R I C B R E I U S M

5. What does the illustration represent?

   FRICTION ——→ FRICTIO ——→ FRICTI ——→ FRICT ——→
   ——→ FRIC ——→ FRI ——→ FR ——→ F ——→
   ——→ O

6. What does the circled letter represent?

   B A L (A) N C E

7. Thrust means to push or drive with force. How can you produce thrust with this combination of numbers and letters?

   2 3 F e O T h

8. What part of a FORCE goes into a golfer's warning to avoid being struck by a ball?

9. If you read a story about two UFOs making contact in flight, what kind of story would this probably be?

10. What does the illustration represent?

    SPEED—→ SDEPE ——→ PSEDE ——→ SEEDP ——→ ESPDE ——→
    ——→ DPSEE

A Mix of Riddles and Problems
(con't)

11. What does the illustration represent?

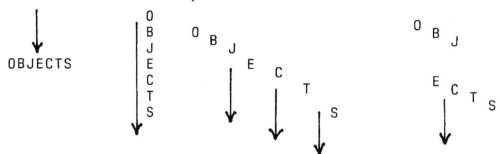

12. What does the illustration represent?

96. Partly There

A. There are 20 physical science terms that are missing three or more letters. The missing parts of the terms are hidden in the puzzle. Find and circle the missing letters. Then place them in the spaces next to the partial terms.

r	a	e	l	e	s	x	f
q	f	a	n	u	a	p	n
x	t	e	b	x	m	r	e
s	i	t	y	o	p	e	d
f	y	e	c	a	r	s	t
m	t	l	d	e	n	s	e
r	a	u	o	s	i	l	r
z	x	c	i	t	e	n	e
t	h	e	r	c	r	y	s
q	f	e	t	i	c	l	z

1. c r y _ _ _ _

2. v o l _ _ _ _

3. _ _ _ _ s t a n c e

4. _ _ _ _ _ _ u r e

5. _ _ _ _ l i t u d e

6. n u c _ _ _ _ _

7. m o l e _ _ _ _ _

8. c o n _ _ _ _ _ _

9. i n t e n _ _ _ _ _

10. _ _ _ _ p o u n d

11. _ _ _ _ _ r g y

12. _ _ _ _ b o n

13. _ _ _ _ _ t r o n

14. l a _ _ _ _

15. m a g _ _ _ _ _ _

16. _ _ _ _ s i t y

17. k i n _ _ _ _ _

18. _ _ _ _ h i n e

19. _ _ _ _ t o p e

20. _ _ _ _ _ m a l

B. Match eight answers from Part A with their two- or three-word descriptions in the right column. Place the letter of the description in the space to the left of the number.

Items From Part A

___ 1

___ 6

___ 10

___ 17

___ 11

___ 4

___ 20

___ 12

Descriptions

a. Moving energy

b. Warm air

c. Atomic energy

d. Air has this

e. Solid, definite form

f. Number six element

g. Two elements chemically combined

h. Heat, sound, and light

Name _____ Date _____

97. Mystery Question Wordsearch

There are 20 scrambled physical science terms and clues. Unscramble them. Then find and circle 10 of the unscrambled terms in the puzzle. The circled terms and shaded areas form five letters. Unscramble these letters and reveal the answer to the mystery question. Terms may be up, down, forward, and diagonal.

a	e	g	r	a	v	i	t	y	r	l	w	s	b	x	f	w
l	z	i	n	c	e	r	e	s	i	n	s	y	v	q	i	a
h	■	■	r	l	b	a	s	e	v	e	m	h	a	s	t	
e	k	m	y	o	r	u	b	b	e	r	b	■	■	s	e	
l	■	■	s	c	q	u	a	r	t	z	o	s	k	i	r	
i	■	j	z	t	i	s	a	l	t	b	p	l	g	w	o	x
u	y	■	n	a	t	f	e	c	h	o	c	s	b	u	n	n
m	i	c	■	l	y	u	l	f	e	■	l	a	s	e	r	
o	x	y	g	e	n	s	e	p	t	m	■	t	y	k	■	g
c	l	i	g	h	t	i	c	■	d	z	■	e	■	v	o	
e	■	q	n	o	■	o	t	■	s	e	o	a	m	h	l	
l	■	l	y	e	■	n	r	c	o	a	l	t	c	u	a	o
l	■	r	o	x	■	w	o	p	h	o	t	o	i	r	o	n
s	o	r	b	i	t	d	n	■	g	f	d	c	i	j		

Scrambled Terms

1. m l i u e h
2. t a w t
3. d a i c
4. e p r m e a
5. u n e t o n r
6. t i g h l
7. r e t a t m
8. t o r i b
9. t o s e l u
10. s i t u l m
11. n o r p o t
12. r y a i t g v
13. o c e h
14. n i s o f i s

Clues

1. Gas; Number 2
2. Unit of electrical power
3. Yields hydrogen ions
4. Unit of electrical current
5. Neutral particle
6. A form of energy
7. Has weight and occupies space
8. Oval path
9. A dissolved substance
10. A dye; indicates acid or base
11. Positive particle
12. Attractive force
13. Reflection of sound
14. Splitting atoms

Mystery Question Wordsearch
(con't)

15. e o l n i h c r
16. n e l r c t e o
17. m l o b y s s
18. g o r d y e n h
19. i c o l y e v t
20. q a p e o u

15. Element Number 17
16. Negative particle
17. Au, K, P, and Ni
18. Lightest substance
19. Speed in a given direction
20. Not able to transmit light

Mystery Question

What do you call a hypothesis that has withstood repeated testing; an explanation backed by experimental results?

— — — — — —

98. Broken Word Maze

Use the clues listed below the puzzle to find the physical science terms hidden in the puzzle. The terms connect to form a trail leading from the *entrance* to the *exit*. Only 15 terms are needed to solve the puzzle. Write the name of the term in the space to the right of the clue. Then draw a line through the term in the puzzle. Keep in mind the terms are *broken*. The first one is done for you.

Entrance

```
q   s   o   j   x   a   l   t   v   v   z   i   o   n   q   j   x   v
z   j   q   l   i   j   v   z   x   q   s   z   v   x   c   r   j   q
i   l   z   v   x   d   q   d   h   e   q   j   x   j   q   e   v   z
z   j   l   v   z   j   a   v   q   z   e   t   t   v   s   q   z   s
m   i   z   q   j   x   q   z   j   v   r   v   a   x   t   j   a   q
q   j   x   v   z   s   y   v   l   a   j   x   v   m   z   j   l   v
z   v   e   e   p   q   z   o   l   j   q   v   r   j   s   v   t   x
q   d   j   z   j   q   x   q   x   j   l   c   u   x   u   j   z   z
v   z   f   r   i   x   j   n   f   u   j   q   m   z   f   x   q   x
j   v   x   z   c   x   o   q   x   z   e   d   v   x   q   v   x   j
q   x   i   t   z   i   j   v   q   i   c   j   q   v   x   t   r   q
z   n   o   j   x   s   j   e   b   v   l   s   i   u   s   x   z   o
j   c   o   z   e   j   q   l   q   e   x   q   j   x   q   v   j   u
q   x   v   h   j   x   w   j   c   v   q   c   x   z   n   e   h   g
z   x   j   x   z   o   v   r   x   z   s   i   v   x   e   q   z   j
x   v   q   k   r   v   e   v   j   i   v   z   g   r   j   v   x   z
q   z   x   p   o   w   j   x   m   x   j   y   j   x   v   q   j   v
```

Exit

© 1995 by The Center for Applied Research in Education

Clues	Term
1. Has definite shape and volume	1. _____ solid _____
2. Has mass and takes up space	2. _____
3. Made up of two or more metals	3. _____
4. Supports a lever; balancing point	4. _____
5. Heat is an example	5. _____
6. Low point of wave	6. _____
7. High point of wave	7. _____

Broken Word Maze
(con't)

8. Another name for centigrade scale   8. _____

9. Unit of sound intensity or loudness   9. _____

10. Moving an object through a distance   10. _____

11. A measure of work   11. _____

12. Molecules bound together   12. _____

13. Rapid movement   13. _____

14. Created by rubbing surfaces   14. _____

15. Holding fast   15. _____

Possible Answers

1. buoyancy
2. isotope
3. laser
4. adhesion
5. cohesion
6. matter
7. energy
8. crest
9. Fahrenheit
10. kilo

11. compound
12. miscible
13. noise
14. friction
15. salt
16. alloy
17. pitch
18. atom
19. Kelvin
20. watt

21. fuse
22. methane
23. power
24. speed
25. solid
26. fulcrum
27. trough
28. Celsius
29. decibel
30. work

99. Group of Four

A. There are 20 four-letter groups of physical science terms below. Write the name of the term in the space under each group of letters.

1. h a		2. d a		3. s l		4. a s		5. i s	
t e		c i		a t		e b		o n	

_____   _____   _____   _____   _____

6. n n		7. k o		8. r x		9. t t		10. t o	
o e		i l		y a		w a		v l	

_____   _____   _____   _____   _____

11. a s		12. z c		13. o r		14. m s		15. w r	
p m		i n		i n		s a		k o	

_____   _____   _____   _____   _____

16. o e		17. k l		18. a o		19. b n		20. s a	
s r		n i		m t		o d		g l	

_____   _____   _____   _____   _____

B. Provide answers for the terms in Part B from the responses in Part A. Place answers in the spaces provided.

1. Metallurgy is the science of taking useful metals from their ores, refining them, and preparing them for use.

    Examples: _____, _____, _____, and _____.

2. Elements are simple substances that cannot be broken down into simpler substances.

    Examples: _____, _____, and _____.

3. These are commonly used terms in measuring electrical energy:

    _____, _____, and _____.

4. Litmus dye indicates the presence of two substances. They are:

    _____, and _____.

5. These three terms are related to atoms. They are:

    _____, _____, and _____.

100. Best Match

Circle the word that best matches the meaning of each physical science term listed below.

Term	Best Match			
1. Metal	ore	slag	sodium	neon
2. Element	neutron	tartanium	glycerine	Neptunium
3. Nonmetal	density	carbon	lead	crystal
4. Neutral Atom	chlorine	water	acid	proton
5. Force	mass	pull	distance	volume
6. Friction	velocity	gravity	speed	rest
7. Water	liquid	hydrogen	oxygen	matter
8. Energy	calorie	kinetic	solid	power
9. Machine	oil	sewing	inertia	pulley
10. Conductor	iron	copper	steel	air
11. Insulator	wax	silver	wire	aluminum
12. Amplitude	trough	crest	base	hertz
13. Music	record	tape	noise	harmony
14. Convex	eye	retina	outward	inward
15. Concave	outward	inward	retina	iris
16. Refract	image	light	eye	bend
17. Atom	newtron	Newton	neutron	compound
18. Voltage	rays	electrons	zinc	cells
19. Thermal	power	energy	heat	velocity
20. Density	time/space	distance/time		mass/volume
21. Ion	proton	charged	neutron	electron
22. Electron	atom	negative	positive	ionic
23. Proton	isotope	ionic	positive	negative
24. Fission	split	fuse	carbonize	oxidize
25. Adhesion	atoms	unlike	particles	anneal
26. Molecule	water	gold	smallest	milli
27. Mass	gold	lead	measure	volume
28. Speed	rate	direction	viscosity	tracer
29. Vacuum	air	space	prism	photon
30. Cohesion	particles	substances	mixture	like

SECTION THREE

Earth Science

Name _____ Date _____

101. Treasures of the Lithosphere

The lithosphere is the outer crust of the earth. Minerals, of course, are found throughout the lithosphere. Let's go on a mineral hunt. Use the hints to complete the name of the minerals.

Hints	Mineral Name
1. Lead ore	_ _ L _ _ _ _
2. Hardness scale, Number 10	_ I _ _ _ _ _ _
3. Used in making powder	T _ _ _ _
4. Rock salt	H _ _ _ _ _ _
5. Hardness scale, Number 4	_ _ _ O _ _ _ _
6. Plaster of Paris	_ _ _ S _ _
7. Pencil lead	_ _ _ P _ _ _ _
8. A type of feldspar	_ _ _ H _ _ _ _ _ _
9. A source of iron	_ E _ _ _ _ _ _ _
10. Fool's gold	_ _ R _ _ _
11. Frozen water	_ _ E

Friendly Challenge

See if you can find . . .
a mineral that has the "hairy coat of a mammal" making up one half of its name.

Answer: _____

a mineral that needs "art" to hold its name together.

Answer: _____

a mineral that mentions the score standard set for each hole of a golf course.

Answer: _____

a mineral with three *e's* in its name; snakelike.

Answer: _____

102. Finding 15 Minerals

Use the clues to help you locate 15 minerals. Write the name of the mineral in the space to the right of the clues.

Clues   Mineral Name

1. Hardness scale, Number 9;
   8 letters   1. c_____

2. This mineral has a "bar"
   in its name; 8 letters   2. c_____

3. You can find "ma" in the
   middle of its name; 8 letters   3. h_____

4. A mineral name that sounds
   like it's always hungry; 7 letters   4. a_____

5. Much of this mineral is involved
   with "rap"; 8 letters   5. g_____

6. You'll find a type of metal in
   this mineral's name; metal's
   name rhymes with skin; 10 letters   6. s_____

7. Most of this mineral suggests
   an opening or exit or entrance
   through a wall or fence; rhymes
   with bait; 5 letters   7. a_____

8. Hardness scale, Number 7;
    6 letters   8. q_____

9. A common European snake makes
   up part of its name; rhymes
   with clasp; 6 letters   9. j_____

10. Two boys' names make up 60
    percent of this mineral's
    name. One boy's name rhymes
    with "con"; the other rhymes
    with "pal"; 10 letters   10. c_____

11. This mineral's name sounds
    like splint; 5 letters   11. f_____

12. Hardness scale; Number 8;
    5 letters   12. t_____

13. The mineral name needs to
    be unscrambled; 8 letters   13. f_____

    o l e f t r i u

14. The major ore of lead;
    6 letters   14. g_____

15. Magnetic; attracts small pieces
    of iron; 9 letters   15. m_____

Name _____ Date _____

103. Gem Mountain

Look at the side of Gem Mountain. There are fragments of nine gem mineral names scattered about. See if you can put them together. Write their complete names in the spaces below the mountain.

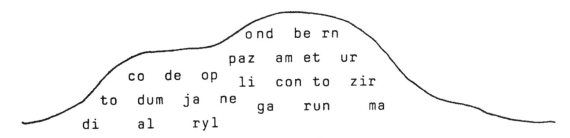

1. _____ (7 letters)   6. _____ (8 letters)

2. _____ (5 letters)   7. _____ (6 letters)

3. _____ (4 letters)   8. _____ (5 letters)

4. _____ (4 letters)   9. _____ (10 letters)

5. _____ (6 letters)

A Bit of Research

Write the name of the "prized gem" that comes from the gem mineral listed below.

Gem Mineral   "Prized Gem"

   1. beryl (blue-green)   1. _____

   2. beryl (deep green)   2. _____

   3. corundum (blue)   3. _____

   4. corundum (red)   4. _____

104. Mineral Maze

Twenty words associated with minerals are hidden in the maze. A definition, description, or example of each word is listed. Circle each word in the puzzle and write it in the space provided. Then draw a line through the Mineral Maze. Start your search at the maze entrance. Your line should be the shortest path possible, should extend from the Entrance to the Exit, and must follow the letters of the circled words in the maze. One answer appears twice in the maze. Answers may be up, down, forward, backward, and diagonal.

ENTRANCE

```
l  e  a  d  b  m  r  a  b  a  n  n  i  c  h
i  k  p  i  c  i  r  p  u  c  s  a  l  t  a
m  t  j  a  o  k  r  e  f  r  a  c  t  s  r
o  v  t  m  k  i  j  l  h  c  a  n  d  r  d
n  r  w  o  l  l  e  y  e  l  s  a  m  u  n
i  q  r  n  i  u  s  p  c  a  i  h  b  s  e
t  u  e  d  e  s  h  i  v  t  m  a  o  t  s
e  a  a  r  q  t  t  g  f  o  c  e  r  m  s
k  r  l  z  i  e  m  e  r  a  l  d  a  o  n
i  t  g  t  v  r  t  m  a  k  r  a  x  i  c
r  z  a  r  p  o  e  f  c  e  v  i  p  r  l
o  t  r  a  s  c  g  h  t  x  c  u  a  z  a
n  o  c  u  i  p  a  w  u  i  l  e  k  y  t
a  i  v  q  s  l  g  a  r  n  e  t  x  a  o
m  l  d  r  i  g  e  t  e  x  a  b  e  y  l
r  o  e  t  i  r  o  u  l  f  v  a  t  i  s
s  f  e  a  s  l  m  a  g  n  e  t  i  t  e  ← EXIT
```

Mineral Maze
(con't)

Word List

1. Chemical symbol, Pb _____

2. Conchoidal, for example _____

3. The color of sulfur _____

4. _____ scale of hardness; 1-10 _____

5. A four-letter word for muscovite _____

6. A gemstone from beryl; green _____

7. A rock-forming mineral _____

8. Number 3 on the scale of hardness _____

9. Resistance to scratching _____

10. Red silicate mineral; usually red crystal _____

11. Number 10 on the scale of hardness _____

12. Calcite bends or _____ light

13. To split or separate _____

14. The appearance of the surface of a mineral in reflected light _____

15. Number 4 on the scale of hardness _____

16. Number 1 on the scale of hardness _____

17. Known as "rock salt" _____

18. Black mineral; attracted by a magnet _____

19. A frozen water mineral _____

20. Number 7 on the scale of hardness _____

105. Where in the Word?

How clever are you at finding hidden words? For example, where in the word *mineral* would you find a word describing an extended period of time? The answer, of course, is era—min*era*l. A word may appear forward or backward.

1. Where is the name of a metal in selinite?

   Answer: _____

2. Where is a plug or stopper in apatite?

   Answer: _____

3. Where is a female servant hiding in a diamond?

   Answer: _____

4. Where is the "entire quantity" in gypsum?

   Answer: _____

5. Where is the gentle or harmless part in hematite?

   Answer: _____

6. Where is the "touch game" in agate?

   Answer: _____

7. Where is the small arachnid in dolomite?

   Answer: _____

8. Where is the "imitation of an original" in chalcopyrite?

   Answer: _____

9. Where is the word that suggests marcasite is "tightly packed"?

   Answer: _____

10. What part of siderite is weary or exhausted?

    Answer: _____

11. What part of galena moves slowly?

    Answer: _____

12. What part of rhodonite hides an immature louse?

    Answer: _____

13. Where is the hotel hiding in cinnabar?

    Answer: _____

14. Where is the sobbing sound of grief in cryolite?

    Answer: _____

Where in the Word?
(con't)

15. Where is a girl's name hiding in uraninite?

    Answer: _____

16. Where is the mineral spring in feldspar?

    Answer: _____

17. Where does a "trip" appear in tourmaline?

    Answer: _____

18. Where does a sharp blow occur in graphite?

    Answer: _____

19. Where are the two animals grazing in wolframite?

    Answer: Animal _____ Animal _____

20. Where is the word that suggests cerussite is positive or certain?

    Answer: _____

21. What word allows you to drink from cuprite?

    Answer: _____

22. What part of opal describes how an animal drinks?

    Answer: _____

23. Where would a central Asian bovine be found in pyroxene?

    Answer: _____

24. Find the saltwater plant in realgar.

    Answer: _____

25. Where in kyanite is the word for denial, refusal, or a negative vote?

    Answer: _____

Name _____ Date _____

106. Twelve Igneous Rocks

Igneous or fire-formed rocks come from molten magma deep within the earth's crust. There are 12 igneous rocks mixed with sedimentary and metamorphic rocks in the three figures below. Locate the igneous rocks and write their names in the spaces provided. Place the number of the rock in the parentheses to the right of the space. The first one is done for you.

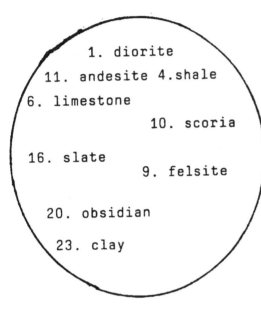

1. diorite
11. andesite   4. shale
6. limestone
10. scoria
16. slate
9. felsite
20. obsidian
23. clay

13. chalk
17. tuff 3. basalt
18. marble
7. gabbro 12. schist
22. syenite

5. rhyolite
19. granite
14. breccia
2. sandstone
15. gneiss
8. dolomite
21. pumice

A. 1. _____diorite_____ (1)   7. _____ ( )

2. _____ ( )   8. _____ ( )

3. _____ ( )   9. _____ ( )

4. _____ ( )   10. _____ ( )

5. _____ ( )   11. _____ ( )

6. _____ ( )   12. _____ ( )

B. Total the numbers of the 12 igneous rocks. The total is _____.

C. Divide 12 into the total from Part B. The answer is _____.

D. Now subtract 0.083333 from the answer to Part C. The answer is _____.

E. What does your answer for Part D have in common with this activity?

_____.

107. Metamorphic Scatter

Metamorphic rocks have been changed from their original form by heat and pressure. For example, shale, a sedimentary rock, changes into slate, a metamorphic rock, when subjected to intense heat and pressure.

    Draw a line connecting the metamorphic rocks scattered below. The line should touch the dots in front of or behind each of the metamorphic rock names. If completed correctly, the line will reveal the answer to the mystery question.

•coquina•
    •soapstone•

    ▪marble•

•serpentine•
    •dolomite•   •quartzite•
    marble

•shale• •schist•   • phyllite•

•granite•
    •graphite•

•gneiss•   •slate•

    •mica-schist•

•limestone•

    • sandstone•   •chalk•

•felsite•

    • gypsum •

    •conglomerate•
    • anthracite •

•bituminous •

    • lignite•

Mystery Question

What earth material is hot enough to change the shape and composition of a rock?

Answer: _____

108. Scrambled Sedimentary Wordsearch

Sedimentary rocks are formed in layers from materials deposited by water, wind, ice, or other agents. There are 10 sedimentary rocks hidden in the puzzle. The letters spelling the name of each rock are scrambled. Find and circle the scrambled rocks in the puzzle. Then write their names in *alphabetical order* in the spaces provided. Use the letter hints to help you. Words may be up, down, forward, backward, and diagonal.

```
c  e  t  o  a  r  e  m  n  l  o  g
i  y  g  u  p  s  m  e
t           a     d              c
l  r  t  e  v  a  r  t  n  i  e  r
h     h     s  l           a     b
a  l     n        a  h           e
e  n  o  t  s  i  l  m  e        i
   t           c        r        c
s              k                 a
```

1. b __ __ c __ __ __ __   6. __ i __ __ s __ __ n __
2. __ h __ l __   7. __ __ __ l
3. __ o __ __ l __ m __ __ a __ __ 8. s __ __ d __ t __ __ __ __
4. __ y __ __ __ m   9. __ h __ __ e
5. h __ __ __ t __   10. t r __ __ __ __ __ i __ e

Research It!

1. What sedimentary rock is used for making writing chalk?
   Answer:

2. What is another name for halite?
   Answer:

3. Slate is the metamorphosed form of what sedimentary rock?
   Answer:

4. What sedimentary rock is a loose, earthy deposit of limestone and clay?
   Answer:

5. This sedimentary rock is composed of fragments of any kind of rock cemented into a solid mass. What is it?
   Answer:

109. Rock Talk

There are 30 words or group of words in the box regarding rocks. Ten words are linked to sedimentary rocks, 10 words relate to igneous rocks, and 10 words are associated with metamorphic rocks. List the words that fit under each of the rock headings listed below.

> granite, batholith, pumice, lava, deposited by water, breccia, shale, ice deposits, layered, laccolith, magma, conglomerate, sand and gravel, schists, heat and pressure, warped crust, slate, tuff, fine banding, folded crust, deposited by wind, foliation, basalt, marble, quartzite, fire origin, limestone, salt, sandstone, and gneiss

Sedimentary Rocks

1. _____   6. _____
2. _____   7. _____
3. _____   8. _____
4. _____   9. _____
5. _____   10. _____

Igneous Rocks

1. _____   6. _____
2. _____   7. _____
3. _____   8. _____
4. _____   9. _____
5. _____   10. _____

Metamorphic Rocks

1. _____   6. _____
2. _____   7. _____
3. _____   8. _____
4. _____   9. _____
5. _____   10. _____

110. Rock Riddles

Let's see how many of the 15 rock riddles you can solve.

1. What do you call the person who is in charge of a university's geology department?

   Answer: _____

2. How can you turn a rock into a cork?

   Answer: _____

3. Mary found a coin in a sedimentary layer of earth. What was the value of the coin?

   Answer: _____

4. Where can silver be found in magma?

   Answer: _____

5. What part of pumice floats the best on water?

   Answer: _____

6. What will this event produce?

   $$\frac{\text{pressure}}{\text{shale}}$$

   Answer: _____

7. What will this event produce?

   $$\frac{\text{pressure}}{\text{limestone}}$$

   Answer: _____

8. Joe and Ellen bought a house made of a metamorphic rock, quartz schist. If Joe wanted to claim part of the house for his very own, what part do you think he would get?

   Answer: _____

9. Four rocks—shale, sandstone, marble, and slate—entered a race. Which rock finished Number One?

   Answer: _____

10. Why does the sedimentary rock, conglomerate, outshine all of the other sedimentary rocks?

    Answer: _____

Name _____ Date _____

Rock Riddles
(con't)

11. Why is the igneous rock, syenite, so popular in Japan?

    Answer: _____

12. Why is the volcanic rock, breccia, always wet?

    Answer: _____

13. A crock holds 23 rocks. A person walks up to the crock and drops in eight more rocks. How many rocks are in the crock?

    Answer: _____

14. Why would anyone call a girl "rocks and pebbles?"

    Answer: _____

15. What does the illustration show?

    Answer: _____

Name _____ Date _____

111. Weathering Challenge

A. Rocks break down in time from the action of weather. This process is known as mechanical weathering. Think about two weathering agents—water and wind—and how they can cause large rocks to crumble into smaller pieces.

Find and circle 13 items in the illustration that help large rocks crumble into smaller rock fragments.

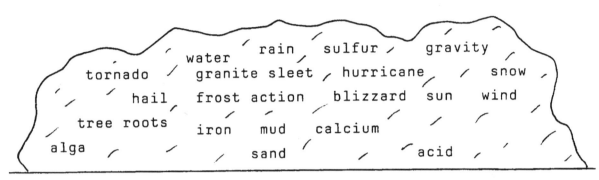

B. The letters of three weathering agents appear in the box. List the agents in the numbered spaces. You must use all of the letters.

```
i  r  o  l
a  s  i  n
n  w  a  h
```

1. _____

2. _____

3. _____

Question: What do all of the weathering agents have in common?

_____

C. The following five words rhyme with objects affected by weathering. List each object in the space to the right of the word.

Words	Objects Affected By Weathering
1. shoulders	1. _____
2. mouse	2. _____
3. toads	3. _____
4. small	4. _____
5. pound	5. _____

Name _____ Date _____

112. Chemical Weathering

Chemical weathering occurs when chemical change takes place. For example, carbonic acid in water can change a mineral like feldspar into a clay mineral by dissolving out certain elements.

A. Unscramble the underlined words in the sentences below. Then write the *unscrambled word* in the space *below* the scrambled word.

1. All chemical weathering processes involve <u>TWRAE.</u>

2. New <u>ESNSCUABTS</u> form during a <u>LEHACMCI</u> change.

3. Water may cause rocks to <u>LESLW</u> and <u>BKERA</u> apart.

4. Carbon <u>DIEXODI</u> and water produce <u>RNBCOIAC</u> acid.

5. Carbonic acid in rain water can, over time, dissolve <u>LSMOTENEI</u> or <u>RAEMBL</u> statues.

6. The chemical process of weathering is known as <u>SPONOICEDMTIO.</u>

7. <u>CYAL</u> forms from the chemical weathering of <u>NIOR</u> or feldspar.

8. Weathering may be a combination of <u>HLMCAIME</u> and <u>CLEMACINAH</u> action.

9. <u>CDIA ANRI</u> helps promote chemical weathering.

10. Acids of <u>LTAPN YECAD</u> dissolve in rainwater and aid in chemical weathering.

B. Fill in the puzzle spaces with answers from Part A.

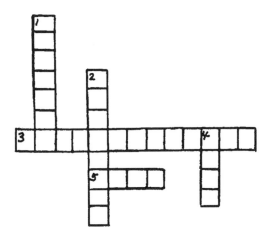

Chemical Weathering
(con't)

Clues

1. An oxide containing two atoms of oxygen in the molecule.
2. Related to chemistry.
3. The act of breaking down through chemical change.
4. A chemical element that readily rusts in moist air.
5. An earthy material containing small particles.

Name _____ Date _____

113. Weathered Objects

A. Use the letters in MECHANICAL and CHEMICAL weathering as the first letters for objects affected by the weathering process. Use the letters in *mechanical* to indicate objects affected by mechanical weathering agents and the letters in *chemical* to indicate objects affected by chemical weathering agents.

M _____   C _____

E _____   H _____

C _____   E _____

H _____   M _____

A _____   I _____

N _____   C _____

I _____   A _____

C _____   L _____

A _____

L _____

B. Now use the letters that spell WEATHERING to produce *five* additional objects that can be mechanically or chemically altered by the weathering process. You may use a letter more than once.

1. _____

2. _____

3. _____

4. _____

5. _____

114. Erosion Wordsearch

Erosion is the gradual wearing away of land surface due to such agents as wind, water, and moving ice. Find and circle 27 terms that relate in some way to erosion. Use the clues listed below the puzzle. Write the puzzle terms in the spaces to the right of the matching clues. Terms may be up, down, backward, forward, and diagonal.

```
t  r  e  s  e  d  a  y  s  r  e  v  i  r  a
s  u  n  o  o  m  t  n  o  y  n  a  c  c  s
u  n  a  i  b  i  a  b  r  e  a  k  e  r  m
n  o  h  o  v  f  l  o  o  d  s  l  m  e  a
o  f  i  a  w  a  t  e  r  f  a  l  l  e  d
i  f  r  g  e  n  i  a  r  o  m  a  a  p  s
t  g  v  i  o  t  e  r  l  d  z  f  n  e  l
i  a  z  m  a  p  r  e  n  c  r  k  d  x  u
s  j  o  l  u  a  c  i  k  e  f  c  s  l  m
o  r  u  e  v  d  w  c  t  w  n  o  l  i  p
p  s  r  i  s  d  f  a  m  i  s  r  i  o  y
e  g  n  a  k  x  w  l  a  e  t  o  d  s  t
d  e  a  y  l  l  u  g  o  p  a  o  e  b  m
n  o  i  s  o  r  e  a  p  w  c  t  i  u  r
t  o  p  s  o  i  l  o  t  q  k  s  a  s  v
```

Clues

1. Soil moving slowly downhill; sounds like jeep. _____

2. Sloping mass of rock fragments below a cliff; sounds like Dallas. _____

3. Large mass of rocks and soil slipping down a mountain side; 9 letters. _____

4. Dry, sandy region; much wind erosion. Begins with the letter *d*. _____

5. Mixture of loose sand, rock, and water moving at a rapid pace; 7 letters. _____

6. Sea wave that breaks on rocks; sounds like faker. _____

7. A deep gorge eroded by water. Begins with the letter *r*. _____

8. A liquid compound of hydrogen and oxygen. _____

9. A deposit of loose material carried and left by a glacier; sounds like terrain.

   _____

10. The uppermost layer of soil; 7 letters. _____

© 1995 by The Center for Applied Research in Education

Erosion Wordsearch
(con't)

11. The wearing away of land surface. _____

12. These structures help anchor plants to the ground. _____

13. A tall, narrow rock formed from wave erosion; sounds like knack. _____

14. Water pouring over a steep slope in a straight-down direction; 9 letters. _____

15. An agent of erosion; moving air. _____

16. A high point of land extending into the ocean; resistant to erosion. The word begins

    with the letter *p*. _____

17. A deep groove in the ground; sounds like bully. _____

18. Large flows of water covering land not usually covered by water. _____

19. The layer of soil below the topsoil; begins with the letter *s*. _____

20. Large, natural streams of water usually leading to the ocean; sounds like slivers.

    _____

21. A large mass of rock that collapses or slides down a sloping surface; sounds like bump.

    _____

22. A large moving mass of ice; begins with the letter *g*. _____

23. Barriers to control the flow of water; 4 letters. _____

24. A force that pulls all objects toward the earth. _____

25. A deep gorge or ravine. The Grand __ __ __ __ __ __. _____

26. Water that runs over the ground; begins with the letter *r*. _____

27. The process of rock particles in water gradually settling as a river slows down; begins with

    the letter *d;* 10 letters. _____

115. Erosion Explosion

Try your luck at avoiding erosion. Play *Erosion Explosion*. It works like this: Place a marker, popcorn kernel or bean, on the game board at the ENTRANCE. Roll a die. Then move the number of spaces on the game board as indicated by the number on the die. For example, if you roll a three, move three steps forward.

Challenge: You have 20 rolls to get through the game board. Each time the marker lands on an agent of erosion—wind, water, etc.—you must add *one* to the total number of rolls. Good luck!

Agents of Erosion

    wind

    water

    glacier

    ocean waves

    river current

    flood

    rain

Erosion Explosion
(con't)

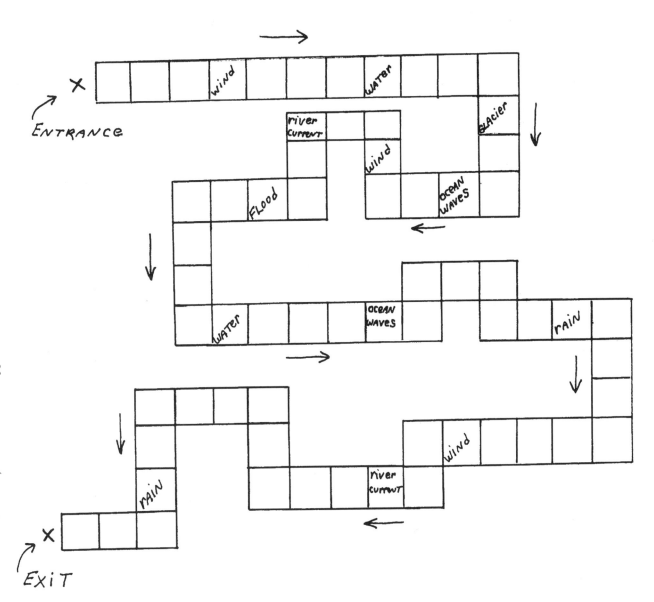

Name _____ Date _____

116. Earth Vibrations

A. An earthquake occurs when a sudden release of energy causes a shaking of the Earth's crust. The stronger the shake, the more damage occurs. Use the two word clues under each box of letters to help you identify terms related to earthquakes. There are two extra letters in each box. Write the term in the space below each box. The first one is done for you.

1.
```
| A |   | U | E |
|   |   |   |   |
| T | F | L | O |
```

break, movement

_____

2.

crust, shake

_____

3.
```
| O | Y | S | E | L | O |
| S | G | M | A | I | E |
```

earthquakes, science

_____

4.
```
| T |   | A |
| C | S | F |
| O |   | U |
```

earthquake, origin

_____

5.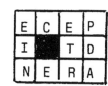
```
| E | C | E | P |
| I |   | T | D |
| N | E | R | A |
```

focus, above

_____

6.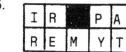
```
| I | R |   | P | A |
| R | E | M | Y | T |
```

waves, fastest

_____

7.
```
| N | A | E | R | D | O |
| I |   | C | Y | S | F |
```

waves, shear

_____

8.
```
| C | T | R | E | A |
| R | L | H |   | I |
```

scale, strength

_____

9.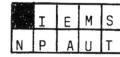
```
|   | I | E | M | S |
| N | P | A | U | T |
```

earthquake, waves

_____

Earth Vibrations
(con't)

B. Combining Terms

1. Use the answers to Numbers 4 and 5, Part A, in a complete sentence.

_____

2. Use the answers to Numbers 1 and 2, Part A, in a complete sentence.

_____

3. Use the answers to Numbers 6 and 7, Part A, in a complete sentence.

_____

C. Matching

Select answers from Part A to match the one-word descriptions below. Write the matching terms in the spaces to the right.

Descriptions	Term
1. sea	1. _____
2. scientist	2. _____
3. origin	3. _____
4. transverse	4. _____
5. longitudinal	5. _____

117. The Big Boom

There are 12 areas marked by numbers on the erupting volcano sketch. Write the names of the volcanic structures and/or volcanic materials on the chart opposite the areas where they would likely be located. There will be more than one item for several areas.

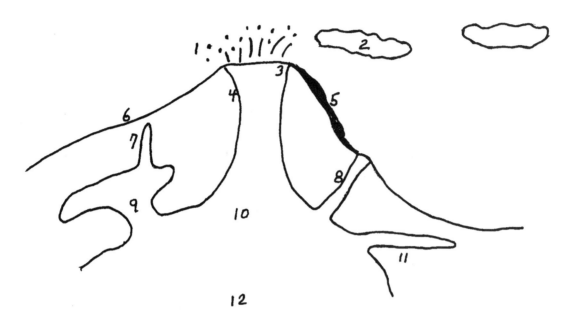

Chart

Volcanic Mountain Sketch	
Area	Structures/Materials
1	
2	
3	
4	
5	
6	
7	
8	
9	
10	
11	
12	

Terms

1. basalt
2. pumice
3. neck
4. lava
5. cone
6. batholith
7. dike
8. sill
9. laccolith
10. cinders
11. gases
12. crater
13. vent
14. magma chamber
15. melted rock
16. side
17. extreme heat and pressure

118. Glacier Mixup

A glacier is a large, slow moving mass of ice and snow. This simple description doesn't offer much information but if you unscramble the statements below, you'll learn more about glaciers. The first one is done for you.

1. cold period ice a is very age An of temperatures.

   An ice age is a period of very cold temperatures. _____

2. ice Glaciers during ages thrive.

   _____

3. about years The age ended ice 11,000 ago last.

   _____

4. climates Glaciers today very in exist cold.

   _____

5. 1,000 feet glaciers thick over many is The ice in.

   _____

6. pressure base of under the great ice The is.

   _____

7. pace Glaciers slow at a move.

   _____

8. glaciers the Gravity move to weight ice of the and cause.

   _____

9. through valleys mountains form in slowly and glaciers downhill move Valley.

   _____

   _____

10. great sheets ice covering glaciers Continental of are a area large.

    _____

    _____

11. floors Glaciers valley out carve.

    _____

12. erosion agents Glaciers of are.

    _____

Glacier Mixup
(con't)

13. rock debris ice of tons Glaciers with carry.

_____

14. till as known silt deposit Glaciers sand and large fragments.

_____

15. A moraine till of glacial a deposit is.

_____

16. edge sheet moraines form End the at ice of the.

_____

17. material deposited Drift its meltwater glacier and by a refers to all the.

_____

_____

119. Earth Features By Design

Use the letters in the 12 words below to design a sketch of how each earth feature might appear. Let your imagination roam. The first one is done for you.

1. volcano

2. fault

3. mountain

4. anticline

5. syncline

6. stalactite

7. stalagmite

8. ravine

9. sediments

10. iceberg

11. plateau

12. submarine canyon

Name _____ Date _____

120. Missing Features

A. Some earth features are listed below; others are missing. Find and circle the missing features in the puzzle. Each feature begins with a different letter of the alphabet. Write the missing terms in the spaces to the right of the letters. Answers may be up, down, forward, backward, and diagonal. *Note:* Omit letters x, y, and z.

```
b  i  d  n  a  l  s  i  n  p  i
a  e  x  r  w  e  a  l  a  r  v
s  c  a  t  u  v  q  w  e  o  k
h  f  m  c  r  e  o  i  c  c  t
c  t  a  g  h  e  c  m  o  k  n
n  v  n  u  i  a  f  z  a  s  e
e  u  t  w  l  o  e  t  c  b  m
r  p  l  g  c  t  d  r  v  l  i
t  l  e  s  a  n  b  a  s  q  d
a  i  t  l  i  v  e  u  f  m  e
q  f  p  w  g  o  r  q  r  u  s
k  t  v  o  l  c  a  n  o  e  n
```

a - abyss

b - _____

c - _____

d - delta

e - exfoliation

f - _____

g - _____

h - hematite

i - _____

j - joint

k - Kilauea

l - _____

m - _____

n - nonmetals

o - _____

p - _____

q - _____

r - _____

s - _____

t - _____

u - _____

v - _____

w - _____

x - omit

y - omit

z - omit

B. List two ways in which the answers to letters q and r are *alike*.

1. _____

2. _____

C. List two ways in which the answers to letters q and r are *different*.

1. _____

2. _____

D. What do the answers to letters g and w have in common?

_____

121. Fossil Candidates

A. Fossils are preserved evidence of past geologic life. There are 10 organisms in the puzzle that, *under the right conditions,* could become fossils. All 10 candidates have two different vowels in combination (eo, iu, oi, etc.) to form their names. Find and circle each one. Names may be up, down, forward, backward, and diagonal.

a	e	d	a	o	t	t	i
y	l	f	e	s	u	o	h
t	r	o	u	t	a	r	o
i	e	i	o	l	n	t	e
u	o	n	i	f	a	o	t
r	e	a	a	o	u	i	a
f	n	e	u	a	g	s	o
s	l	b	a	u	i	e	g

List the names of the organisms in the spaces below according to the letter combinations in parentheses.

1. _____ (ai)   6. _____ (ua)

2. _____ (ea)   7. _____ (oi)

3. _____ (ea)   8. _____ (ui)

4. _____ (oa)   9. _____ (oa)

5. _____ (ou)   10. _____ (ou)

B. As mentioned in Part A, an organism may become fossilized *under the right conditions.* Generally, if an organism has hard parts and becomes quickly buried, it stands a chance of becoming a fossil. List six organisms from Part A that have the *best* chance of turning into a fossil.

1. _____   4. _____

2. _____   5. _____

3. _____   6. _____

C. Why would a trout stand a better chance of becoming a fossil than an apple?

_____

_____

D. Paleontology is the study of fossil remains. Use the letters in PALEONTOLOGY to spell the names of six different organisms that could become fossils. You may use a letter more than once.

1. _____   4. _____

2. _____   5. _____

3. _____   6. _____

122. Organisms Found As Fossils

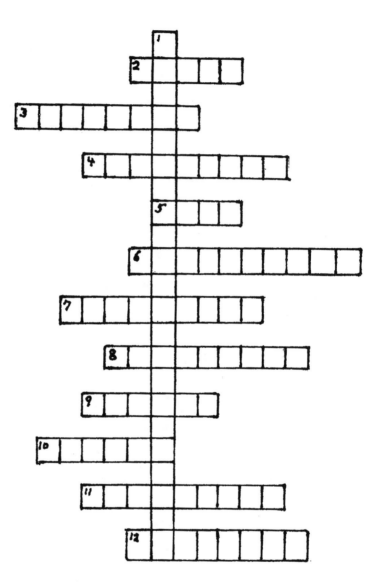

Organisms Found As Fossils
(con't)

Across

2. Skeletal deposits from various polyps; helps build reefs and islands.

3. A five-armed echinoderm.

4. A "three-lobed" marine arthropod.

5. Cold-blooded aquatic animal.

6. A marine invertebrate with two unequal shells or valves.

7. Mammal with a pouch on the female for carrying the young.

8. Class of mollusks; snail, for example.

9. A member of the phylum Porifera.

10. Palm-like tropical evergreen plants.

11. Flat, spiral shells; abundant in the Mesozoic era.

12. Alligators, turtles, and snakes are good examples.

Down

1. A sedimentary rock containing fossils.

123. 10 Mysterious Dinosaurs

The dinosaur names come in sections. Part of the names are listed below. The remaining pieces are hidden in the puzzle. Find and circle the missing parts. Then complete the names by filling in the blank spaces. Answers may be up, down, forward, backward, and diagonal.

```
d   r   e   p   t   r   i   e   o   t
o   d   o   n   e   g   y   s   y   l
c   f   u   t   n   w   t   r   o   t
u   t   i   o   y   e   a   s   w   i
s   r   d   a   g   n   a   t   c   c
y   o   h   o   n   u   s   h   a   h
r   a   p   y   r   o   t   l   y   t
w   v   m   u   k   h   g   x   j   h
e   i   s   i   g   u   a   n   s   y
```

1. _ _ _ _ _ _ osaurus

2. diplo _ _ _ _ _ _

3. anky _ _ _ _ _ _ _ _

4. _ _ _ ceratops

5. _ _ _ _ _ saurus

6. trach _ _ _ _

7. _ _ losaurus

8. dimet _ _ _ _ _

9. _ _ _ _ _ odon

10. _ _ _ _ _ _ osaur

Mystery Question: Dinosaur skeletons and footprints have been found in a sedimentary rock made up of a loose material. What is the name of the loose material? *Hint:* Four letters of DINOSAUR go together to spell its name. _____

Name _____ Date _____

124. Bits and Pieces

Four fossils—starfish, crinoid, brachiopod and ammonite—were resting in their sedimentary beds. Then, over hundreds of years, a steady increase of heat and pressure caused them to twist, stretch and break into pieces.

Here is the BEFORE...

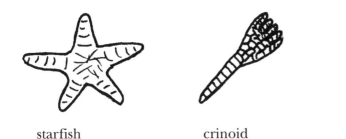

starfish   crinoid   brachiopod   ammonite

Here is the AFTER...

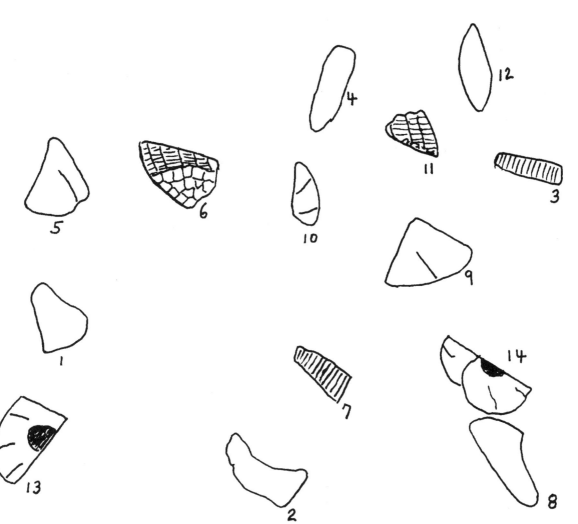

Bits and Pieces
(con't)

Try to put the fossils back together by placing the numbers of each fossil piece into its respective box below. For example, if pieces 3, 4, 8, and 9 went together to complete the ammonite, then these numbers would go into the box labeled ammonite.

<table>
<tr>
<td>

</td>
<td>

</td>
<td>

</td>
<td>

</td>
</tr>
<tr>
<td>starfish</td>
<td>crinoid</td>
<td>brachiopod</td>
<td>ammonite</td>
</tr>
</table>

Mystery Question: A metamorphosed fossil is one that has undergone heat and pressure. Due to this tremendous stress and strain, the fossil may not be recognizable. What two natural events may cause a fossil to be altered?

1. _____

2. _____

125. Fossil Riddles

Try your luck at solving the following 10 riddles:

1. What ancient invertebrate has a bite but no teeth?

   Answer: _____

2. What does this sketch represent?

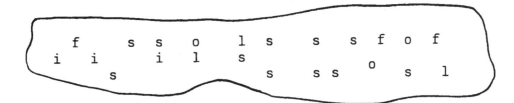

   Answer: _____

3. Gigantic elephants roamed the earth millions of years ago. Some have been found frozen in glaciers. What insect appears each time someone discovers one of these mammals?

   Answer: _____

4. People seldom hear about the discovery of dried, fossilized animal remains. Why is this?

   Answer: _____

5. If your cat or dog became fossilized, in what condition would it appear?

   Answer: _____

6. What do you call a fossilized tree with evidence of burned bark?

   Answer: _____

7. Dinosaur fossils are found in many areas, including Wyoming and Utah. In what state do geologists find most of the invertebrate (animals with no backbone) fossils?

   Answer: _____

8. What make-believe music company might produce songs with the following titles?
   "Don't Jostle The Colossal Fossil"
   "A Cast At Last"

   Answer: _____

Fossil Riddles
(con't)

9. If you found strange organisms preserved in rock dated back 20 million years, what word might come to mind?

20-million-year-old rock

Answer: _____

10. Karen found a poorly preserved fossil snail. What part of the snail was in the weakest condition?

Answer: _____

Name _____ Date _____

126. Clouds About

Clouds are condensed moisture suspended in air molecules. Clouds form as moisture condenses around dust particles.

A. Place a check mark (✓) to the right of ten terms below that relate in some way to clouds, for example: names of cloud formations, their effect on the environment, and so on.

s k y	s t r a t ⓤ s
m e t e o r i t e	c ⓞ p p e r
ⓒ o r a l	q u a r t z
w i n d s	ⓝ i m b u s
c o n d e n ⓢ a t i o n	s i l i c a
c u m u l u s	p r e c i p i t a t i o n
ⓑ a s a l t	s e d ⓘ m e n t
m o i s t ⓤ r e	t h u n d e r s t o r ⓜ s
f a ⓤ l t	g y p s u ⓜ
f o s s i l	s ⓛ e e t

B. Use the underlined letters in Part A to spell the name of wispy, high clouds consisting of ice crystals.

_ _ _ _ _ _

C. Use the circled letters in Part A to spell the name of thunderhead cloud masses known to produce thunderstorms.

_ _ _ _ _ _ _ _ _ _ _ _

D. In *four words or less* tell how these paired terms relate.

1. cumulus and stratus

_____

2. moisture and sleet

_____

3. thunderstorms and winds

_____

4. precipitation and nimbus

_____

Clouds About
(con't)

E. Find and circle *five words* below that, when placed next to each other in the correct order, would explain why rain falls to the earth.

moisture   mixed   rise   condenses   fluffy   light   heavy   shape   temperature
clouds   droplets   ocean   fall   dry   absorbs

Now place the words in their correct order. Use the number of spaces to help you put the five words in their correct order.

_ _ _ _ _ _ _ _   _ _ _ _ _ _ _ _ _ _ ;   _ _ _ _ _ _

_ _ _ _ _ _ _ _   _ _ _ _.

127. Tornado Power

Use the clues to help you find the correct answers to the puzzle. Begin with Number One at the bottom of the puzzle and work your way to the top. The answers follow in order.

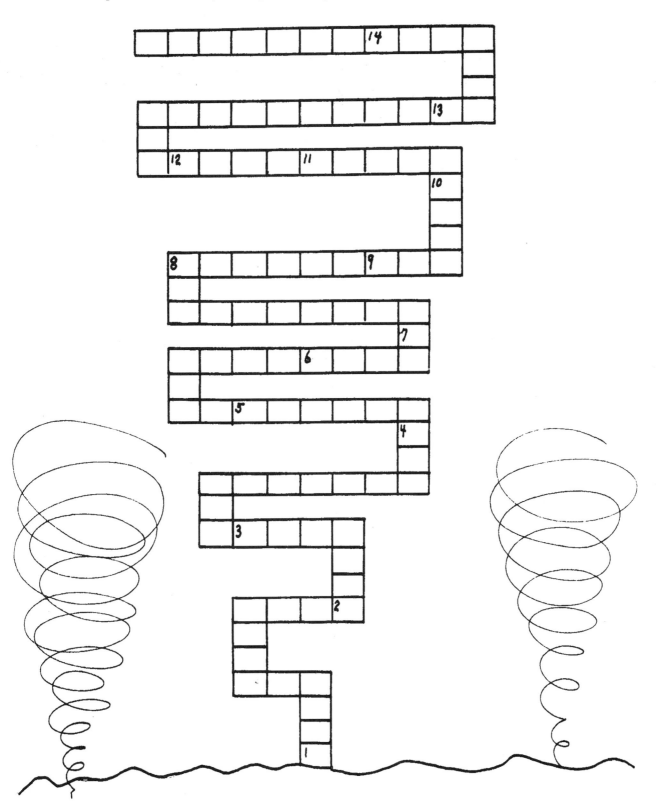

Tornado Power
(con't)

Clues

1. These tornadoes form over water (two words).

   w __ __ __ __   s __ __ __ __ __

2. There are many tornadoes in this state.

   K __ __ __ __ __

3. The area where many tornadoes occur (two words).

   t __ __ __ __ __ __   b __ __ __

4. The shape of a spinning tornado cloud.

   f __ __ __ __ __

5. A tornado moves with a s __ __ __ __ __ __ __ __ motion.

6. Most tornadoes strike during the middle or l __ __ __ afternoon.

7. Tornadoes destroy e __ __ __ __ __ __ __ __ __ __ in their paths.

8. Tornadoes usually touch g __ __ __ __ __ for only a few minutes.

9. Tornadoes are the most powerful storms on e __ __ __ __.

10. A tornado may occur on a hot, h __ __ __ __ day when the sky is filled with thunderclouds.

11. A tornado travels in a wandering p __ __ __.

12. Winds in a tornado's funnel may reach 500 m __ __ __ __ p __ __ h __ __ __.

13. The average life of a tornado is about 15 m __ __ __ __ __ __.

14. The winds in a tornado may also be described as moving in a circular or

    w __ __ __ __ __ __ __ motion.

© 1995 by The Center for Applied Research in Education

Name _____ Date _____

128. Twenty Weather Terms

A. Definitions or descriptions for 20 different weather terms appear below. Only a part of each term is revealed. Find the missing part for each term in the box and write it in the spaces provided.

hum	Torri	rus	cum	wea	ont
oud	wa	psych	sation	thun	int	cli
wi	meter	precip	storm	see	anemo
fr	celli	torn	ezes	thunder	ther
	sle			stre	

1. The daily conditions of the atmosphere. __ __ __ ther

2. The temperature at which conden __ __ __ __ __ __ occurs is called the

    dew po __ __ __.

3. A __ __ __ rm __ __ ont develops when a warm air mass meets a cold air mass.

4. __ __ __ idity is moisture in the atmosphere.

5. __ __ nd is air in motion.

6. Thin, white, feathery clouds consisting of ice crystals are classified as cir __ __ __.

7. __ __ __ mate is long-term weather.

8. An instrument called an __ __ __ __ __ meter measures wind speed.

9. Land and sea bre __ __ __ __ result from unequal heating of land and water.

10. A __ __ __ __ __ rometer is used to measure humidity.

11. __ __ __ atus are low, foglike clouds.

12. __ __ __ ulus are puffy, pillow-like clouds.

13. Cl __ __ __ __ __ __ ding is an artificial way of producing precipitation from clouds.

14. Rain is an example of __ __ __ __ __ __ itation.

15. A fr __ __ __ is the boundary between two air masses.

16. A baro __ __ __ __ __ measures air pressure.

17. Temperature is measured with a __ __ __ __ mometer.

18. __ __ __ __ der is the loud sound that follows a flash of lightning.

19. Frozen or partly frozen rain is known as __ __ __ et.

20. A __ __ __ __ ado is a small, violent storm with strong winds.

Twenty Weather Terms
(con't)

B. There are four groups of letters remaining in the box. Put them together and answer these questions:

1. Who invented the barometer?

   — — — — — — — — — —

2. What type of storm originates in cumulonimbus clouds?

   — — — — — — — — — — — —

Name _____ Date _____

129. Weather Word Scramble

A. Use the listed clues to help you fill in the blank spaces with the correct letters. Words may appear forward or backward.

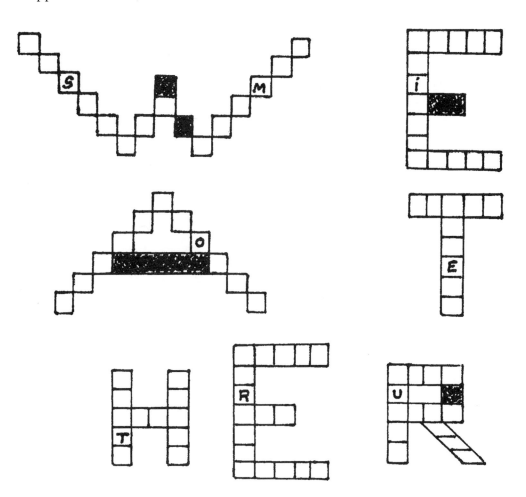

1. A raincloud (6 letters).

2. The condition of material closely packed together (5 letters).

3. Forms of matter without definite shape or volume (5 letters).

4. Milky white clouds consisting of ice crystals (6 letters).

5. A core of high speed winds: jet _____ (6 letters).

6. Solid form of water (3 letters).

7. A fine spray of tiny water droplets (4 letters).

8. Protects Earth against ultraviolet rays (5 letters).

9. Cumulus and nimbus are two examples (6 letters).

10. Rain in a half-frozen state (5 letters).

11. Small drops of precipitation (7 letters).

12. A mixture of oxygen and nitrogen (3 letters).

Weather Word Scramble
(con't)

13. Large body of salt water (3 letters).

14. A planet undergoing various weather and climate changes (5 letters).

15. A collection of moving air (5 letters).

16. Moist, damp atmospheric conditions (5 letters).

17. Wide, thin cloud layers (7 letters).

18. Small masses of frozen rain drops (4 letters).

19. Large areas of air; may stay in place for long periods of time (6 letters).

20. A form of precipitation (4 letters).

21. State of matter having a definite shape and volume (5 letters).

B. Use five of the eight letters provided in the puzzle to answer this question: What word describes a disturbance in the normal condition of the atmosphere?

Answer: __ __ __ __ __

Name _____ Date _____

130. Figure It Out

Let's see how many of the following items you can solve. Be creative. Flexible thinking is the key to success.

1. What do these eight letters represent?

   cy   cy   cy   cy

   Answer: _____

2. What do these paired groups of letters represent?

   cli   cli

   Answer: _____

3. Think of a way to show that *water* makes up about 71 percent of weather.

   Answer: _____

4. How many *winds* can you create from the letters below?

w	n	d	b	n
w	i	n	e	d
e	e	n	i	w
r	w	z	d	i

   Answer: _____

5. What does the illustration represent?

   W   W
       I   I
              N
          D   D
    S   S

   Answer: _____

6. What do you think this means?

   calm ——————▶ storm

   Answer: _____

Figure It Out (con't)

7. What does the sketch represent?

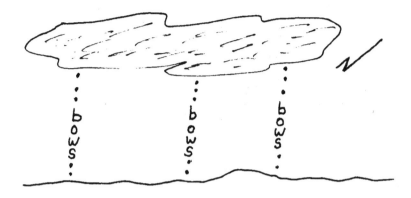

Answer: _____

8. What do drizzle and sleep have in common?

Answer: _____

9. What does this mean?

saturation   ⟶ •

Answer: _____

10. What do you think this means?

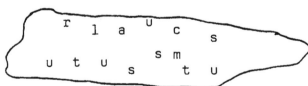

Answer: _____

11. What do you think this represents?

Answer: _____

12. Guess what this is?

Answer: _____

Name _____ Date _____

131. Sea Life

The sea teems with plant and animal organisms. Find and circle the 10 organisms in each sketch below that live in the sea. List the organisms in *alphabetical order* in the spaces to the right of each sketch.

A.

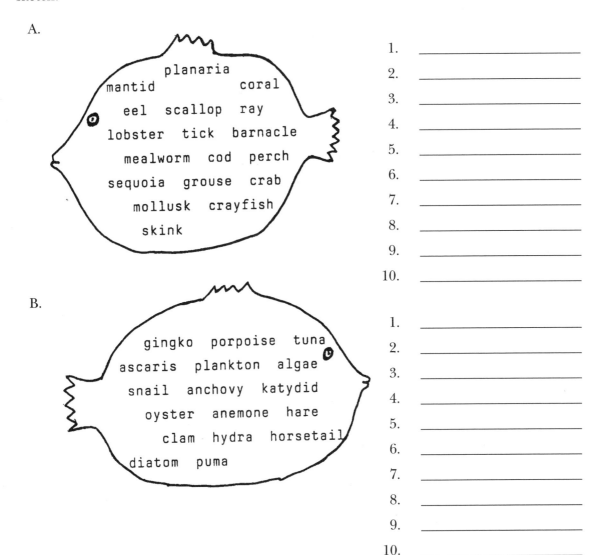

planaria
mantid   coral
eel scallop ray
lobster tick barnacle
mealworm cod perch
sequoia grouse crab
mollusk crayfish
skink

1. _____
2. _____
3. _____
4. _____
5. _____
6. _____
7. _____
8. _____
9. _____
10. _____

B.

gingko porpoise tuna
ascaris plankton algae
snail anchovy katydid
oyster anemone hare
clam hydra horsetail
diatom puma

1. _____
2. _____
3. _____
4. _____
5. _____
6. _____
7. _____
8. _____
9. _____
10. _____

C. List the sea organisms from Part A that use fins for locomotion.

_____

D. List the sea organisms from Part B that are considered fit for human consumption.

_____

E. List the sea organisms from Parts A and B that have a hard outer covering for protection.

Part A _____

Part B _____

132. Hidden Treasure

Oceanographers are scientists who study the ocean and its contents. If you successfully complete the following puzzle (with the help of the limerick), you will find the answer to the mystery question. Use the clues to complete the terms related to the ocean.

Clues	Term
1. seamount; flat top	1. __ __ y __ __
2. volcanoes, earthquakes; giant sea waves	2. __ s __ __ __ __ __
3. water; rise, fall	3. __ __ __ __
4. ocean floor; deep fissure	4. __ r __ __ __ __
5. coral reef; circular	5. __ __ __ l __
6. plant; red, green	6. __ __ g __ __
7. low point; wave	7. t __ __ __ __ __
8. high point; wave	8. __ r __ __ __
9. fine sediment; sea floor	9. __ __ z __
10. ocean floor; shallow	10. s __ __ __ __
11. fast-moving water; wind	11. c __ __ __ __ __ __
12. depression; ocean bottom	12. __ __ __ __ n
13. ridge of coral; water	13. __ __ __ f
14. surrounded by water; land	14. i __ __ __ __ __

Mystery Question

What do you call the device used for detecting submerged objects?

Answer: _____

Limerick

There once was a fisherman Scot,
who knew a most secretive spot;
He'd fish night and day,
This King of Fillet,
and also could follow a dot.

© 1995 by The Center for Applied Research in Education

Name _____ Date _____

133. Undersea Mystery

There are 14 items related to oceanography listed below. Each item has three possible answers. Underline the number/letter combination you feel is correct. Then find the number/letter combination on the chart and place a dot where they intersect. Connect the dots with a line and the pattern will reveal the answer to the mystery question.

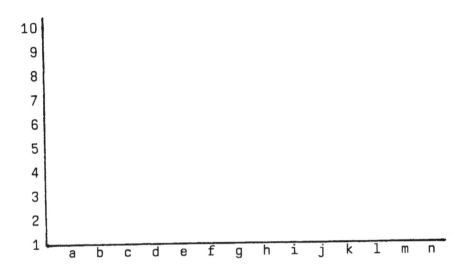

1. A series of underwater mountains. (trenches - 10g, atoll - 4b, mid-ocean ridges - 6e.)

2. Scientists who study the ocean. (oceanographers - 1m, botanists - 5c, marineologists - 10e.)

3. An undersea object or structure. (atoll - 3h, submarine - 1b, pedalfer - 7j.)

4. Deep sea floor gash. (turbidity zone - 5n, trench - 4d, continental shelf - 8d.)

5. Giant sea waves produced by earthquakes or volcanic action on the sea floor. (rip currents - 4m, refractions - 5i, tsunamis - 1n.)

6. A strong, forceful flow of water. (coriolis - 2d, current - 7h, continental drift - 9m.)

7. The low point of a sea wave. (trough - 1l, crest - 8c, undertow - 5h.)

8. The high point of a sea wave. (refraction - 9k, crest - 1a, fetch - 4h.)

9. A series of rocks at or near the surface of water. (continental slope - 2i, guyot - 4f, reef - 2c.)

10. A sea mammal. (octopus - 8k, nautilus - 9a, manatee - 4j.)

11. A zone of rapidly increasing depth. (continental slope - 7f, continental shelf - 8m, barrier reef - 9d.)

12. The distance between crests of a wave. (longitude - 9j, latitude - 6m, wavelength - 2k.)

13. Plant and animal sea life. (trilobite - 6m, plankton - 6i, pelecypods - 3l.)

14. An apparatus for detecting underwater objects and structures. (radar - 6l, sonar - 8g, radiosonde - 5m.)

Mystery Question

What undersea structure does the profile on the chart suggest?

Answer: __ __ __ __ __ __ __

134. The Big Eight

There are eight mini-problems to solve. Use your creative thinking ability to help you find the answers.

1. How many *waves* can you find in the box?

    ```
    e w w s v w
    a s e s a v
    v e s w e s
    a v e a v e
    w a v s a w
    ```

    Answer: _____

2. What would a LOBSTER be if the letters BER disappeared?

    Answer: _____

3. What is the condition of the sea water?

    $$\frac{tow}{strong}$$

    Answer: _____

4. Diatoms are microscopic one-celled plants. They are abundant in fresh and salt water. What is the smallest particle of a diatom?

    Answer: _____

5. Jellyfish and sea anemones belong to the *coelenterate* group. Find another sea animal in the coelenterate group. *Hint:* The name begins with a *c*, has five letters, and is "hiding" in the word coelenterate.

    Answer: _____

6. Show how salt makes up one-half of a BARNaCLE.

    Answer: _____

7. Use an arrow ( ) to show how to get a *seahorse* out of a *seashore*.

    Answer: _____

8. What do the words represent?

    ```
    a
    n
    boat
    boat
    c
    e
    a
    n
    ```

    Answer: _____

135. The Ocean Floor

A. Find and circle the 17 terms listed below in the puzzle. Each term is related in some way to the ocean bottom. Terms may be up, down, forward, backward, and diagonal.

```
s   c   s   e   g   d   i   r   n   a   e   c   o   d   i   m
t   o   d   n   o   o   m   p   i   a   m   l   w   s   f   e
a   n   v   a   l   l   e   y   s   f   v   s   t   g   y   n
r   t   k   j   o   b   t   k   m   a   t   n   i   z   k   s
s   i   c   p   i   l   u   c   c   i   u   z   e   a   e   x
n   n   l   o   u   p   r   h   e   o   t   s   o   o   i   g
i   e   m   a   z   u   y   l   m   k   r   i   n   n   t   u
a   n   f   q   s   a   p   a   o   x   r   a   b   w   e   y
t   t   a   t   g   e   e   n   e   k   c   e   a   p   v   o
n   a   b   y   s   s   a   l   p   l   a   i   n   i   e   t
u   l   v   u   p   l   u   t   o   p   h   q   m   a   r   g
o   s   f   s   u   n   e   v   a   t   r   k   s   e   o   a
m   h   m   t   c   r   a   c   k   s   s   l   n   r   v   o
s   e   d   i   m   e   n   t   s   a   d   c   s   a   w   j
h   l   e   j   d   h   t   r   a   e   h   f   l   c   b   i
v   f   k   m   t   s   t   h   e   l   e   n   s   a   m   a
e   p   o   l   s   l   a   t   n   e   n   i   t   n   o   c
```

abyssal plain
continental shelf
continental slope
cracks
crust
fault
guyot
lava
mid-ocean ridges

mountains
rift zone
rock
seamounts
sediments
trench
valleys
volcanoes

B. Moving left to right, from Point A to Point B, identify the sea floor structures in the diagram.

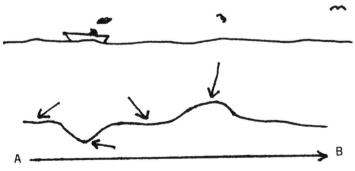

Answers: _____, _____, _____, _____.

C. What do the letters in the box spell?

Answer: _____

```
S  H  T  O
L     H  A
```

136. Coal Game

Coal is a fossil fuel. It forms from the remains of such plants as mosses and ferns that lived long ago. Coal is a nonrenewable energy source because it is used up faster than it can form.

Peat, lignite, bituminous (soft coal), and anthracite (hard coal) is the order in which coal develops. Let's see if you can play Coal Game and win!

Here are the rules:

- Play alone or challenge a fellow classmate.
- Use a marker (a bean, for example) to move along the game board.
- Flip a coin. If heads appear, move *four* spaces. If tails appear, move ahead *two* spaces.
- You must land on *each* of the four coal stages at least *once* to win.
- You have 12 coin flips to win.
- If you land on a coal stage you already have, no gain.
- If you land on an empty space, no gain.
- If you land on a "lose a stage" space, you must remove a coal development stage you've hit before. For example, if you have two peats and land on a "lose a stage," you must forfeit all of the peats.
- If you cross the finish line *before* you have gained all four stages, you lose the game.
- If you gain all four stages of coal development *before* you cross the finish line or *before* the 12 coin flips, you win the game.

Game Board Symbols

     P = Peat

     L = Lignite

     B = Bituminous (soft coal)

     A = Anthracite (hard coal)

Coal Game
(con't)

GAME BOARD

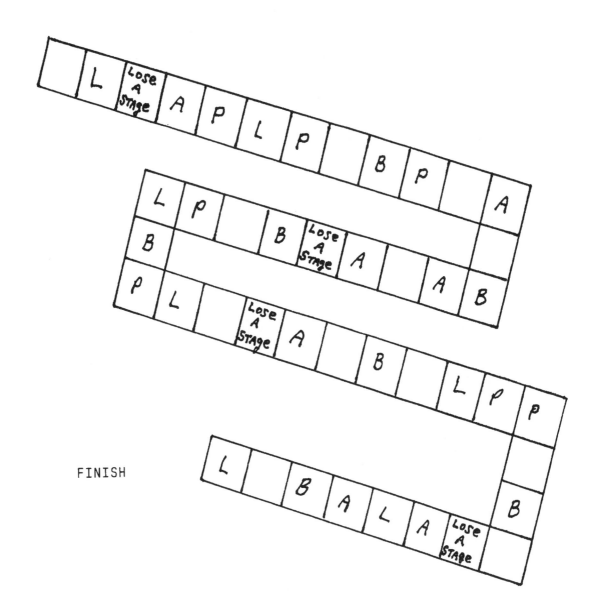

START

FINISH

Name _____ Date _____

137. Mini-Problems

Use your creative problem-solving ability on these eight mini-problems concerning nonrenewable energy sources.

1. Show what coal looks like under pressure.

2. Which stage of coal—peat, lignite, bituminous, or anthracite—catches fire the easiest? Why do you think so?

3. If you remove a letter from COAL, the word COAL would disappear. How can this be?

4. Show how three fourths of dirt is made up of petroleum.

5. How many times does gas appear in the puzzle? There are 20 letters. You may use a letter only *once*.

    s   l   g   a   p
    o   a   e   g   s
    s   t   r   a   g
    u   m   g   s   e

6. What does the illustration show?

7. Rearrange the symbols and letters to spell the name of a stage of coal development.

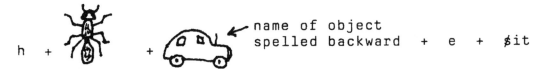

h + 🐜 + 🚗 ← name of object
                 spelled backward + e + ¢it

8. Underline the words below that describe a *nonrenewable* energy source.

    dousedthuprefasterdithanoitpcanlwbesureplacedwbypnatureoant

138. Disappearing Materials

A. Once the Earth's materials—metals and nonmetals—are used up, we'll have a major problem to solve.

There are several metals and nonmetals hidden in the puzzle. Some names appear more than once. Lightly darken the letters that spell the name of each metal and nonmetal. If you do so correctly, the remaining letters can be unscrambled to answer the Bonus Question. Names may be up, down, forward, backward, and diagonal.

s	d	l	o	g	c	e	s
a	i	t	o	r	o	g	u
n	o	l	s	a	p	r	l
d	d	a	v	v	p	a	f
s	n	r	n	e	e	v	u
d	e	o	■	l	r	e	r
i	r	o	n	g	o	l	d
i	c	o	p	p	e	r	r

B. Use *six* letters in NONRENEWABLE RESOURCES to spell the name of a radioactive energy source. You may use a letter more than once.

_ _ _ _ i _ _

Bonus Question

What is a seven-letter synonym for RENEW?

_ _ _ _ _ _ _

139. Going, Going . . .

Fill in the missing letters to complete the names of non-renewable materials. Use the clues to help you find the answers.

Nonrenewable Materials

1. _ _ n _
2. _ _ o _ _ _ _
3. _ _ _ _ n _
4. _ r _ _
5. _ e _ _ _ _ _
6. n _ _ _ _ _
7. _ e _ _

   w

8. _ _ a _ _ _
9. b _ _ _ _ _ _
10. _ _ _ _ l _ _ _
11. _ _ _ _ e _
12. _ _ _ _ m _ _ _ _ _
13. _ _ a _ _ _ _
14. _ _ _ _ t _ _ _
15. _ e _ _ _ _ _
16. _ _ _ _ r _ _ _ _
17. _ i _ _ _ _ _
18. _ _ a _
19. _ _ l
20. s _ _ _ _ _

Clues

1. loose granular material
2. heavy gas, C_3H_8
3. lead ore
4. chemical symbol, Fe
5. gas, CH_4
6. chemical symbol, Ni
7. stage of coal development
8. loose rounded rock fragments
9. aluminum ore
10. motor fuel
11. chemical symbol, Cu
12. soft coal
13. nuclear reactor fuel
14. iron ore
15. chemical symbol, Hg
16. hard coal
17. stage of coal development
18. organic sedimentary rock
19. greasy liquid substance
20. chemical symbol, Ag

140. Nine Boxes

There are nine boxes with letters to spell the answer to each of the items regarding nonrenewable energy sources. There is one extra letter in each box. When you have completed the names, use the nine extra letters to spell the answer to the mystery question.

1. A combination of carbon and hydrogen.

o	c	n	d
m	h	r	r
a	o	y	b

_ _ _ _ _ _ _ _ _

2. Something formed from plants and animals millions of years ago. (two words)

f	s		f
e	o	u	l
l	o	i	s

_ _ _ _ _ _   _ _ _ _

3. A black sedimentary rock that burns.

a	o	e
	l	c

_ _ _ _

4. The name for hard coal.

	a	l	t
i	h	n	e
a	c	r	t

_ _ _ _ _ _ _ _ _ _

5. The name for soft coal.

o	n		u
t	s	i	o
u	m	b	i

_ _ _ _ _ _ _ _ _ _

6. The environment for coal-forming plants.

	m	s	w
a	s	r	p

_ _ _ _ _ _

7. Where crude oil is separated into useful products.

y	i	f
e	r	e
t	n	r

_ _ _ _ _ _ _ _

8. A type of fuel; rhymes with magazine.

n	r	e
e	k	p
o	e	s

_ _ _ _ _ _ _ _

© 1995 by The Center for Applied Research in Education

Nine Boxes
(con't)

9. Another name for brown coal.

i	t	g	e
e	n	l	i

_ _ _ _ _ _ _

Mystery Question

What do you call an oily flammable liquid made up mostly of carbon and hydrogen? *Hint:* It is a source of gasoline.

_ _ _ _ _ _ _ _ _

141. Fun With the Sun

A. The sun is a renewable energy source because it constantly produces solar energy. Twenty words or names that rhyme with terms related to the sun are listed below. Write the matching term in the space to the right of each word.

Word	Term	Word	Term
1. contusion	1. _____	11. allergy	11. _____
2. connection	2. _____	12. decision	12. _____
3. scare	3. _____	13. car	13. _____
4. mellow	4. _____	14. stratosphere	14. _____
5. night	5. _____	15. nation	15. _____
6. molar	6. _____	16. Einstein	16. _____
7. Ramona	7. _____	17. mass	17. _____
8. cesium	8. _____	18. forget-me-not	18. _____
9. dominance	9. _____	19. street	19. _____
10. Michigan	10. _____	20. troposphere	20. _____

B. Unscramble the following six terms.

Scrambled	Unscrambled
1. wloyle	1. _____
2. ennsihus	2. _____
3. rtsa	3. _____
4. mleuhi	4. _____
5. nhoyregd	5. _____
6. gyrene	6. _____

C. Place the *unscrambled* terms 1, 2, and 3 from Part B in a complete sentence.

_____

D. Place the *unscrambled* terms 4, 5, and 6 from Part B in a complete sentence.

_____

142. Water Words

Water is a renewable energy source and covers about 70 percent of the Earth's surface. Find and circle in the puzzle 24 terms that relate in some way to water.

```
r  f  f  o  n  u  r  r  e  s  y  e  g  j  s  t
i  m  u  n  d  e  r  g  r  o  u  n  d  u  u  h
v  g  i  t  b  v  y  a  b  i  d  e  i  p  n  r
e  h  f  s  e  a  e  w  c  r  r  l  o  i  a  e
r  a  i  n  t  p  f  e  g  e  i  b  x  t  r  e
i  h  y  d  r  o  g  e  n  i  z  a  y  e  u  t
a  k  j  o  g  r  d  k  i  c  z  e  g  r  n  w
r  l  l  e  w  a  r  a  r  a  l  m  e  p  r  e
e  p  m  a  e  t  s  l  p  l  e  r  n  l  u  l
v  s  n  o  w  e  c  e  s  g  x  e  y  u  t  v
i  e  t  a  t  i  p  i  c  e  r  p  a  t  a  e
r  c  o  n  d  e  n  s  a  t  i  o  n  o  s  s
a  l  l  i  g  a  t  w  h  a  l  s  h  a  r  l
i  o  w  a  m  o  n  t  s  t  r  e  a  m  w  i
```

Alphabetize the circled terms in the puzzle. Also, to the right of each term, indicate in parentheses the phase of matter. For example, *L* for *Liquid*, *G* for *Gas* and *S* for *Solid*. The first one is done for you.

1. _____bay (L)_____   13. _____

2. _____   14. _____

3. _____   15. _____

4. _____   16. _____

5. _____   17. _____

6. _____   18. _____

7. _____   19. _____

8. _____   20. _____

9. _____   21. _____

10. _____   22. _____

11. _____   23. _____

12. _____   24. _____

Name _____ Date _____

143. Five Renewable Energy Sources

Renewable energy sources include the sun, wind, water, forests, and air. Use the first letter in the name of these sources as the first letter in the answer to each of the following items.

1. The moon, for example. s _ _ _ _ _ _ _

2. The seventh planet from the sun. u _ _ _ _ _

3. The sub-atomic particle with no electric charge. n _ _ _ _ _ _

4. Daily atmospheric conditions. w _ _ _ _ _

5. Fire-formed rock. i _ _ _ _ _ _

6. A gas or dust cloud in space. n _ _ _ _ _

7. The weight per unit volume of any material. d _ _ _ _ _ _

8. Air in motion. w _ _ _

9. Hard coal. a _ _ _ _ _ _ _ _ _

10. Another name for a tidal wave. t _ _ _ _ _ _

11. Removal of soil and rock fragments by natural agents. e _ _ _ _ _ _

12. Earth materials make these. r _ _ _ _ _

13. Preserved evidence of past life. f _ _ _ _ _ _

14. Study of sea and its characteristics. o _ _ _ _ _ _ _ _ _ _ _

15. The bending of a light wave. r _ _ _ _ _ _ _ _ _

16. Large subdivision of the geologic time scale. e _ _

17. Sixth planet from the sun. s _ _ _ _ _ _

18. A funnel-shaped, violent storm. t _ _ _ _ _ _

19. Refers to the sun. s _ _ _ _ _

20. Smallest particle of an element. a _ _ _ _

21. An electrically charged atom. i _ _

22. The circling of one object about another. r _ _ _ _ _ _ _ _ _

144. Renewable Energy Mini-Problems

See how many of the ten mini-problems you can solve using your creative thinking ability.

1. How can you make SUN into a five-letter word?

2. What does the sketch represent?

```
    W       W
        I
    N       N
  D           D
```


3. How can three letters spell water?

4. What does the sketch represent?

5. What does the number and letter combination represent?

    $4 + Fe\ 0$

6. What type of energy comes from the illustration?

$$\frac{ground}{steam}$$

7. What does the sketch represent?

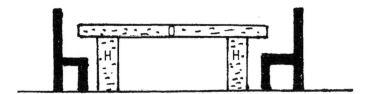

8. What do the mixed letters suggest?

    s w a i n d w r e t n u

9. George Collier had an unusual hobby. He would look for the word SOLAR in magazine and newspaper articles. Every time he came across the word, he'd cut it out and put it in a shoe box. His friends would describe George with these words:

    "George is a human __ __ __ __ __ __ __ __ __ __ __ __ __ __ __."

Renewable Energy Mini-Problems
(con't)

10. What is the meaning of the following series of repeated words?

   renewable energy sources; renewable energy sources;

   renewable energy sources; renewable energy sources;

   renewable energy sources; renewable energy sources;

   and so on

145. Can You Find Them?

A. Wind is a renewable energy source. Draw a line through the five words that relate to the wind. Words may be FORWARD, BACKWARD, and DIAGONAL.

```
t   a   i   r   t   e
o   a   c   l   i   m
e   z   e   e   r   b
d   b   s   h   a   p
n   o   i   t   o   m
```

List the words in the spaces below.

1. _____   4. _____

2. _____   5. _____

3. _____

B. Water is a renewable energy source. Draw a line through the five words that relate to water. Words may be UP, DOWN, and BACKWARD.

```
a   t   w   u   i   o   w
f   e   o   e   h   l   e
d   i   l   o   s   f   t
a   c   f   b   i   d   m
t   n   e   r   r   u   c
g   d   i   u   q   i   l
```

List the words in the spaces below.

1. _____   4. _____

2. _____   5. _____

3. _____

C. The sun is a renewable energy source. Draw a line through the five words that relate to the sun. Words may be FORWARD, BACKWARD, and DIAGONAL.

```
y   g   r   e   n   e   g
e   s   f   b   j   u   a
k   o   a   l   o   i   m
c   l   i   g   h   t   d
h   f   u   n   a   o   l
e   c   l   i   p   s   e
```

List the words in the spaces below.

1. _____   4. _____

2. _____   5. _____

3. _____

Name _____ Date _____

Can You Find Them?
(con't)

D. The forest is a renewable energy source. Draw a line through the five words that relate to a forest. Words may be UP, DOWN, and FORWARD.

```
t   r   o   p   i   c   a   l
w   o   o   d   p   f   s   c
i   c   h   t   l   j   e   a
e   k   l   e   a   v   e   s
b   m   a   u   n   p   r   g
k   o   r   l   t   w   t   d
r   n   o   t   s   l   o   r
```

List the words in the spaces below.

1. _____   4. _____

2. _____   5. _____

3. _____

Name _____ Date _____

146. Plenty of Planets

This is a three-part puzzle. For Part One, unscramble the letters to form the name of a planet. Write the name of the planet in the empty space below the letters. *Note:* There are two extra letters in each group.

Part One

```
      T                    S                   O   P
  A   U                       A            E   U
                      R   N                       T
    R   E              N       R            L   A
  R   S   N          M
```

_____   _____   _____

```
    U                      T                 E   N   T
  I   R   S              A   R               P   N   T
                      T   H   E              U   E   R
  P   J   E                  R
    T   X
```

_____   _____   _____

```
  E   I   R              V   A   E           U   S   A
    E   R   M                S   T             N   A   U
      C   U   Y           U   N
                                               L   R
```

_____   _____   _____

Part Two: List the planets in order from their distances from the sun. Number One would be the closest to the sun.

1. _____   6. _____

2. _____   7. _____

3. _____   8. _____

4. _____   9. _____

5. _____

Plenty of Planets
(con't)

Part Three: Use the two extra letters from each circle (a total of 18) to write the answer to this question:

Volcanoes have been discovered on the moon and planets. What would the volcanic cone, Olympus Mons, on the planet Mars be considered?

Answer: (two words) __ __   __ __ __ __ __ __ __ __ __ __ __ __ __ __ __ __!

© 1995 by The Center for Applied Research in Education

Name _____ Date _____

147. Mr. Sol

The Latin name for sun is *sol*. Let's have some fun with Mr. Sol.

The statements are examples or descriptions for words containing the letter group *sol*. Write the matching word in the space to the right of each example or description. Underline *sol* in the word. The first is done for you.

Example or Description

1. Remote; a lonely place.   1. _____*sol*itude_____

2. No life anywhere; barren.   2. _____

3. To offer comfort to someone.   3. _____

4. To find an answer; to clear up a problem.   4. _____

5. A serious expression.   5. _____

6. To set free or forgive.   6. _____

7. A liquid substance that dissolves another substance. 7. _____

8. To break up into small particles.   8. _____

9. Past tense of sell.   9. _____

10. To separate from others.   10. _____

11. A dissolved substance; sugar in

    hot coffee, for example.   11. _____

12. A system of planets, moons, etc.,

    revolving around the sun.   12. _____

13. A one-person card game.   13. _____

14. To beg for food or request money.   14. _____

15. Flying alone in an airplane.   15. _____

16. To make firm or strengthen.   16. _____

17. To support a grief-stricken person.   17. _____

18. Rude behavior toward someone.   18. _____

19. Perfect or pure.   19. _____

20. The beginning of summer or winter

    in the northern hemisphere.   20. _____

21. _____, liquid and gas.   21. _____

22. A cousin of the flounder.   22. _____

23. Used as a motor fuel.   23. _____

24. An answer to a problem.   24. _____

25. A member of the military, especially army.   25. _____

26. No longer in use.   26. _____

148. The Moon

Tems to describe the examples or definitions below are scattered over the face of the moon. Put the terms together by combining the scattered single or grouped letters. Cross out the letters as you find each term. Then write the term in the appropriate spaces.

```
      cho   re   ma   cus
   wax  moon  ca   lu   me
   tion  noes  o   vo   ing
   Ty   or   ses   se   pres   sa
   clip  rite  be   bit   quake
  per  ite  e   ni   do   cent
   nar  cra  al   lu   sion
  Co  te  de  wan  cres  pha
    ing  vol  tell  ria  ter
```

Moon Terms

1. _____
2. _____
3. _____
4. _____
5. _____
6. _____
7. _____
8. _____
9. _____
10. _____
11. _____
12. _____

Examples or Descriptions

1. The percentage of light reflection from the moon.
2. A saucer-like depression on the surface of the moon.
3. A term referring to the moon.
4. The name of a moon crater (10 letters).
5. A celestial body orbiting another of larger size.
6. The phase immediately following new moon.
7. A dimming of light from one heavenly body by another.
8. New Moon, First Quarter, Full Moon, for example.
9. The name of a moon crater. Begins with the letter T (5 letters).
10. Openings from which hot steam, gases, ashes, etc., are ejected.
11. A low or sunken surface feature.
12. A meteor that strikes the moon's surface.

The Moon
(con't)

13. _____ 13. Large stretches of dark sand and dust scattered over the moon's surface.

14. _____ 14. Crustal disturbances on the moon.

15. _____ 15. The path taken by the moon as it travels around the earth.

16. _____ 16. The moon as it approaches fullness.

17. _____ 17. The opposite of waxing.

149. Planetary Puzzle

There are 30 words related to planets in the solar system hidden in the puzzle. Find and circle each word. Then alphabetize them in the spaces below the puzzle. Words may be up, down, forward, backward, and diagonal.

a	b	e	m	l	i	g	h	t	s	u	n	e	v	k
t	l	g	z	n	a	e	o	b	r	e	t	u	o	t
m	o	o	n	s	s	z	v	e	y	m	e	t	u	m
o	i	n	n	e	r	a	t	j	x	o	s	y	r	c
s	a	t	e	l	l	i	t	e	t	s	a	v	a	s
p	f	s	y	i	p	z	e	u	l	a	h	x	n	n
h	i	k	h	u	r	d	l	x	r	l	p	o	u	i
e	s	y	j	y	d	p	e	s	g	n	i	r	s	a
r	o	r	b	i	t	h	s	r	l	t	o	p	q	l
e	s	u	n	f	t	k	c	f	o	m	a	s	s	p
u	r	c	t	r	e	p	o	m	c	t	l	w	y	e
n	a	r	a	z	m	b	p	v	h	e	b	o	r	p
o	m	e	n	u	t	p	e	n	c	l	o	u	d	s
a	i	m	t	i	a	l	p	s	r	e	t	a	r	c

Alphabetize the words in the spaces below.

1. _____   11. _____   21. _____

2. _____   12. _____   22. _____

3. _____   13. _____   23. _____

4. _____   14. _____   24. _____

5. _____   15. _____   25. _____

6. _____   16. _____   26. _____

7. _____   17. _____   27. _____

8. _____   18. _____   28. _____

9. _____   19. _____   29. _____

10. _____   20. _____   30. _____

150. Space Bits

Below are ten astronomical mini-puzzlers. If you can solve seven of them, you are a "space genius" of celestial quality.

1. Why does *terrestrial* appear twice?

   terrestrial   terrestrial

   _____

2. Spell the name of a satellite, a planet, and a self-luminous gaseous celestial body from the letters in ASTRONOMY. You may use a letter more than once.

   _____

3. What feature can be found in the center of Jupiter? _____

4. The sketch below shows what all inner or terrestrial planets have in common. What is it?

   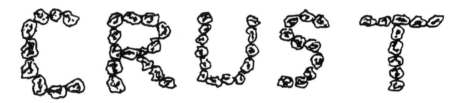

   _____

5. The two identical words below describe what Venus has been called with reference to the Earth. What is it?

   EARTH
   EARTH

   _____

6. What solid, rocklike extraterrestrial exists because of a steroid?

   _____

7. What does the sketch represent?

   m   e   t   e
              t   i
                    e   o   r

   _____

Space Bits
(con't)

8. What does the sketch represent?

_____

9. During what phase does the moon work the hardest?

_____

10. What four letters of the alphabet are responsible for the origin of a star?

_____

ANSWER KEY

Section One: Life Science
The Cell

1. All About Cells

   1. chloroplasts 2. centrioles 3. membrane 4. protoplasm 5. DNA 6. nucleolus 7. mitochondrion 8. cellulose 9. organelles 10. ribosome 11. vacuole 12. cytoplasm 13. chromatin 14. diffusion 15. carbon dioxide.

   Mystery Question Answer: ribonucleic acid

2. Structures of the Plant Cell

   Across: 1. cell 4. rectangular 6. nucleus 8. chlorophyll 9. cytoplasm 11. ribosomes 12. vacuoles.

   Down: 1. cellulose 2. reticulum 3. mitochondrion 5. chloroplasts 7. photosynthesis 10. green.

3. Rhyming Cell Terms

   1. cell 2. life 3. membrane 4. cytoplasm, protoplasm 5. centriole 6. tissue 7. chlorophyll 8. diffusion 9. osmosis, mitosis, nucleolus 10. fission 11. mitosis, osmosis, nucleolus 12. vacuole 13. chloroplast 14. nuclei 15. organelle 16. cytology 17. Hooke 18. respiration 19. cell wall 20. gene.

4. Two Clues

   1. nucleus 2. osmosis 3. mitochondria 4. rna 5. plant cell 6. chromatin 7. vacuole 8. mitosis 9. dna 10. nucleolus 11. diffusion 12. chloroplast 13. cell wall 14. lysosomes 15. protoplasm.

   Bonus Question: ccnilue = nucleic

5. Putting It All Together
   Plant Cell: chloroplasts, cell wall, nucleus, cytoplasm, vacuole and ribosomes.
   Animal Cell: nucleolus, cytoplasm, vacuole, nucleus, centriole and mitochondrion.

Genetics

6. Twenty of Thirty

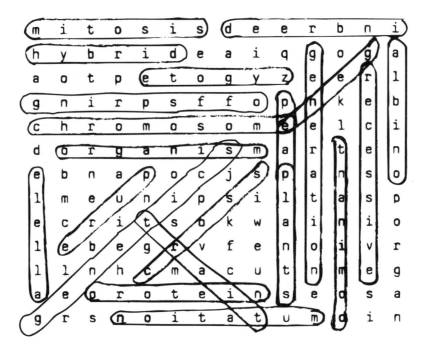

Alphabetical Order: 1. albino 2. allele 3. chromosome 4. cross 5. dominant 6. gene 7. generation 8. genetics 9. hybrid 10. inbreed 11. mitosis 12. mutation 13. offspring 14. organism 15. pea plants 16. protein 17. pure 18. recessive 19. trait 20. zygote.

Possible answers for brief descriptions: albino - lacking pigment 2. hemophilia - bleeding disorder 3. heredity - passing characteristics 4. zygote - fertilized egg 5. gene - hereditary unit 6. offspring - organism progeny 7. mitosis - cell division.

7. Missing Letters

1. *heredity* 2. *dominant* 3. *recessive* 4. *trait* 5. *chance* 6. *inherit* 7. *probability* 8. *cross* 9. *ratio* 10. *hybrid*.

Answers to questions: 1. genetics 2. traits 3. genes 4. gamete 5. chance

Mystery Question Answer: genes.

8. Great Traits

Bony Fish: pectoral, bladder, scales, gills, and vertebrate.

Flower: anther, ovary, sepals, pistil, and petals.

Paramecium: gullet, groove, vacuole, cilia, and conjugation.

A Challenge: shape, texture, and color.

9. It's Too Crowded

1. Sutton 2. gamete 3. peas 4. Mendel 5. first 6. offspring 7. recessive 8. dominant 9. trait 10. chance 11. ratios 12. square 13. hybrid 14. pure 15. generation 16. heredity 17. genetics 18. second 19. dihybrid 20. monohybrid.

10. Genetic Mini-Puzzlers

    1. The word "end" is in the middle of M*end*el.

    2. The word *some* - chromo*some*.

    3. *Recess*ive

    4. Four (seven little x's and one large X inside the box)

    5. i, s, r, t, a, and t = traits

Evolution

11. Mr. D

    A. 1. species - circle i 2. fossils - circle w 3. mutation - circle d 4. evolve - circle n 5. variations - circle a 6. extinct - circle r.

    B. Darwin

    C. Seven

    D. Five

12. Scattered Fragments

    1. muta 2. men 3. ange 4. sils 5. ti 6. pl 7. sur 8. ation 9. grad 10. test 11. evi 12. nct 13. envir 14. mals 15. ge.

    Mystery Question Answer: Jean Baptiste de Lamarck.

13. The Strong Ones

    Answers will vary. Here are some possible responses:

    N - carnatio*n* (last letter), *n*ewt (first letter) A - *a*lga, tun*a* T - *t*urnip, *t*iger U - spr*u*ce, lem*u*r R - *r*adish, *r*am A - pot*a*to, arm*a*dillo L - aza*l*ea, *l*izzard S - *s*ycamore, manti*s* E - alo*e*, *e*el L - *l*otus, came*l* E - ros*e*, ant*e*ater C - *c*arrot, *c*od T - *t*ulip, oys*t*er I - end*i*ve, car*i*bou O - beg*o*nia, *o*tter N - cor*n*, *n*autilus.

14. Change Through Time

    1. oyster 2. spider 3. flower 4. sponge 5. insect 6. turtle 7. rodent 8. spruce 9. mussel 10. monkey 11. walrus 12. ginkgo.

15. Evolution Cre-Eight-Ives

    1. Change through time.

    2. Offspring.

    3. Evolution of the horse.

    4. Selection #5 because this would be a "natural selection."

    5. Punctuated equilibrium.

    6. The first four letters—evol—spelled backwards is love, a score of nothing in tennis.

    7. Three different theories.

    8. Rat - mig*rat*ion.

Plants

16. Mixed Up Plants

   A. 1. taproot 2. pith 3. cambium 4. cuticle 5. root 6. stoma 7. epidermis 8. phloem 9. xylem 10. stalk 11. cork 12. cortex.

   B. 1. stoma 2. cambium 3. xylem 4. cortex 5. cuticle.

   C. carnivorous plant.

17. It Begins With An S

   Across: 1. spongy 3. stamen 4. sunflower 5. squash 9. sporophyte 10. stem 11. seedling 12. spruce 13. sepal 14. stigma 15. stimuli

   Down: 1. sprout 2. seed 3. sprig 4. sequoia 6. spores 7. soil 8. style 10. sphagnum 11. stomata 12. sunlight.

18. Four Squares

Puzzle #1:	moss (top); scum (right side); Mars (bottom); stem (left side).
Puzzle #2:	algae (top); cone (right side); fern (bottom); algin (left side).
Puzzle #3:	forest (top); desert (right side); ground (bottom); grow (left side).
Puzzle #4:	mineral (top); leaves (right side); lichen (bottom); xylem (left side).

19. Vascular Plants

   1. violet 2. daisy 3. rose 4. spruce 5. club moss 6. tulip 7. cycad 8. horsetail 9. pine 10. palm 11. cedar 12. ginkgo 13. cactus 14. iris 15. redwood 16. corn 17. fern 18. oak 19. orchid 20. tomato 21. peach.

20. Fruit Mini-Puzzlers

   1. 4 (fig, fruits, peach and tomato or orange).

   2. One (There is only one *i* to spell fig).

   3. None. The word *fruits* begins with the letter *f*.

   4. One possibility is A - avocado, B - bean and C - cucumber.

   5. $\dfrac{\text{mature}}{e}$ + seeds   A fruit is a mature ovary (over e) plus seeds.

   6. Fruit stand.

   7.   f
      a p r i c o t
           g

Invertebrates

21. Worms Are Invertebrates

   a 9, b 10, c 3, d 16, e 17, f 2, g 6, h 13, i 4, j 5, k 15, l 11, m 14, n 12 and o 7.

   Mystery Question Answer: heartworm

22. Land-Dwelling Invertebrates

    Puzzle Answers: aphid, bee, caterpillar, centipede, cicada, dragonfly, earthworm, hookworm, leech, millipede, mite, mosquito, moth, nematode, planaria, snail, sowbug, tapeworm, tick and trichina.

    Groupings: *Insects:* aphid, bee, caterpillar, cicada, dragonfly, mosquito, and moth. *Arachnids:* mite and tick. *Myriapods:* millipede and centipede. *Mollusks:* snail. *Isopoda:* sowbug. *Segmented Worms:* earthworm and leech. *Round Worms:* hookworm, nematode and trichina. *Flatworms:* planaria and tapeworm.

23. Insects Everywhere

    1. bee 2. cricket 3. ant 4. ladybug 5. termite 6. flea 7. June beetle, mayfly 8. walking stick 9. planthopper, grasshopper, leafhopper, grass flea 10. cricket 11. mantid or mantis 12. cockroach 13. stonefly 14. earwig 15. bed bug 16. cicada 17. beetle 18. horse fly 19. wasp 20. bumble bee.

    The cricket appears twice in the puzzle.

24. Invertebrates At Sea

    1. jellyfish 2. snail 3. starfish 4. squid 5. sea urchin 6. hermit crab 7. shrimp 8. brain coral 9. ribbon worm 10. nautilus 11. octopi 12. isopod 13. sea squirt 14. limpet 15. chiton.

25. Times Up!

    Item One: bee and ant; Item Two: bat or rat; Item Three: bee; Item Four: bee, weevil and beetle; Item Five: jellyfish, cuttlefish or starfish; Item Six: No backbone; Item Seven: The five worms spell the word "worms." Therefore, five worms plus the spelling of worms equal six.

Vertebrates

26. Vertebrate Equipment

    A. 1. c 2. a 3. b 4. a 5. c 6. d 7. b 8. a 9. d 10. a.

    B. Body Structures: 1. caudal fin - tail fin of fish; 2. operculum - gill cover of fish; 3. tympanum - eardrum of frog; 4. pectoral fin - fin of fish, next to head; 5. nictitating membrane - eyelid of frog; 6. crop - stomach of bird; 7. syrinx - throat area of bird; 8. femur - large leg bone of frog, man; wing bone of bird; 9. sternum - breastbone of frog, bird, and man; 10. ulna - upper limb or arm bone of frog, man; wing bone of bird; 11. patella - kneecap of man.

27. Half and Half

    1. allig + ator = alligator 2. arma + dillo = armadillo 3. chee + tah = cheetah 4. chip + munk = chipmunk 5. copper + head = copperhead 6. du + gong = dugong 7. her + ring = herring 8. le + mur = lemur 9. mon + key = monkey 10. opos + sum = opossum 11. pir + anha = piranha 12. platy + pus = platypus 13. por + poise = porpoise 14. rab + bit = rabbit 15. sand + piper = sandpiper 16. spar + row = sparrow 17. tor + toise = tortoise 18. tua + tara = tuatara 19. tur + key = turkey 20. tur + tle = turtle.

    Bonus: Diamondback Rattlesnake

28. Enter the Mammal

    1. cheetah 2. ocelot 3. marten 4. Letter h 5. bear 6. rabbit 7. deer 8. rodent 9. skunk 10. raccoon 11. opossum 12. Letter f 13. marmoset 14. Letter h 15. lemur 16. beaver 17. ferret 18. whale 19. bat.

    Item #1: a four-chambered heart

    Item #2: ram and rat

    Item #3: hare

    Item #4: doe

29. Mystery Vertebrate

    1. cod 2. lizard 3. kangaroo 4. cormorant 5. dolphin 6. bass 7. bat 8. moose 9. lion 10. toad 11. porcupine 12. robin.

    Item Answers: A. cod, dolphin, and bass. B. cormorant, bat, and robin. C. lizard, kangaroo, moose, lion, porcupine, and toad.

30. What Is It?

    1. ant 2. ark 3. rat 4. rib 5. gnu 6. gill 7. ash 8. nasa (NASA) 9. hero 10. dill 11. ton 12. bad 13. toy 14. pin 15. ease 16. skin 17. cod 18. new 19. ant 20. lie.

Human Skeleton

31. Skull Session

    1. *Cranial bones:* 1. ethmoid 2. frontal 3. occipital 4. parietal 5. sphenoid 6. temporal.

    2. *Facial bones:* 1. lacrimal 2. mandible 3. maxilla 4. nasal 5. palatine 6. vomer.

    3. mandible and maxilla

    4. tears

    5. occipital bone

32. Limb, Hand, and Foot Bones

    Horizontal answers from top to bottom: ulna, calcaneus, fibula, and cuboid. *Vertical answers* from left to right: patella, phalanx, femur, talus, radius, humerus, and carpal.

    Ligament, shIn, Muscle, Bone, Skin; tHumb, pAlm, kNuckle, inDex; Fungus, buniOn, tOe, Tarsal.

33. Bones in a Box

    Box answers: 1. spine 2. atlas 3. ilium 4. pubic.

    Four circle letters: ribs

    Sketch answers: 1. rib 2. sternum 3. vertebra 4. sacrum 5. ilium.

    Horizontal answers from top to bottom: vertebra, ilium; *Vertical answers* from left to right: sternum, rib, sacrum.

    Mini-puzzler answer: They all represent *bones*. Part b shows the numbered letters of the alphabet - 2 = b, 15 = o and so on.

34. Mixed Bag of Bones

    1. cranium 2. femur 3. shinbone 4. radius, ulna 5. humerus 6. patella 7. breastbone 8. xiphoid process 9. mandible 10. ankle.

    Big Bone Bonus Answer: The words in the puzzle indicate a skull and crossbones. The skull and crossbones serve as a symbol of death, as a warning label on poison, and as an emblem of piracy.

    Bone Letters Answer: You can spell BONE only once. Two or more spellings would make it plural - BONES.

35. Bones Galore!

    1. sacrum 2. scapula 3. vomer 4. clavicle 5. coccyx 6. lumbar 7. thoracic 8. cervical 9. axis 10. manubrium 11. phalanges 12. metacarpal 13. ulna 14. patella 15. ischium 16. maxilla 17. zygomatic 18. fibula 19. sphenoid 20. radius.

    What Do You Think? Thoracic Park.

    What Do You Think? Mr. Tarsal "metacarpal."

Human Body Systems

36. ABC's of Human Body Structures

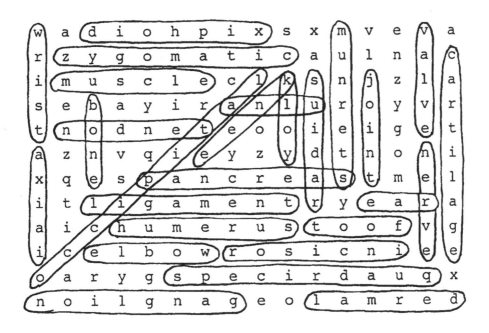

axial; bone; cartilage; dermal; elbow or ear; foot; ganglion; humerus; incisor; joint; knee; ligament; muscle; nerve; occipital; pancreas; quadriceps; radius; sternum; tendon; ulna; valve; wrist; xiphoid; yolk; zygomatic.

37. Support and Movement

1 PELVIS
2 LUMBAR
3 SPINE
4 TARSALS
5 RIBS
6 BONES
7 ULNA
8 CARPAL
CERVICAL
9 KNEE
10 PERIOSTEUM
11 AXIAL
12 CARTILAGE
13 TIBIA
14 HUMERUS
15 APPENDICULAR
16 FIBULA
17 TENDON
18 STERNUM
19 MANDIBLE
20 ARTHRITIS
21 SACRUM
22 RADIUS
23 SCAPULA
24 CA
25 HIP
26 VERTEBRAE
27 CLAVICLE
28 ILIUM
29 SHIN
30 MAXILLA
31 ARM
32 JOINT
33 THORACIC
34 ISCHIUM
35 CRANIUM
36 SHAFT
37 FEMUR
38 ELBOW
39 PHALANGES
40 ATLAS
41 MARROW
42 AXIS
43 METATARSAL

38. Which Way Out of the Bone Maze?

39. Digestion, Respiration, and Reproduction

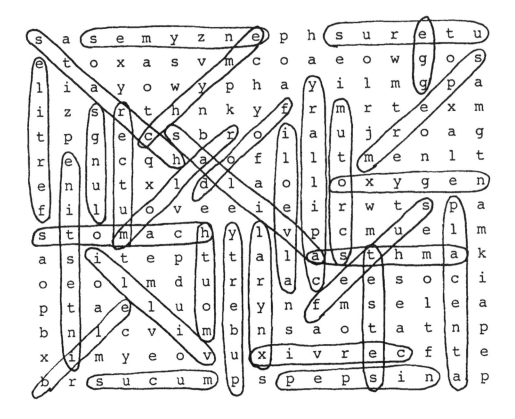

anus	embryo	molar	rectum
alveoli	enzymes	mouth	saliva
asthma	feces	mucus	scrotum
bile	fertile	ovaries	sperm
breathe	fetus	oxygen	starch
bronchi	food	pancreas	stomach
capillary	intestine	pepsin	testes
cervix	larynx	pharynx	trachea
chyme	liver	placenta	uterus
egg	lungs	puberty	villi

TERMS: 1. mucus 2. fertile 3. larynx 4. alveoli 5. molar 6. pepsin 7. chyme 8. bile 9. stomach 10. asthma

40. Staying in Circulation

1. aorta 2. four 3. smooth 4. veins; atrium 5. heart; ventricles 6. valves 7. diffusion 8. large 9. pulmonary 10. carotid 11. type O 12. fibrin 13. white blood 14. hemoglobin 15. plasma 16. red blood 17. capillaries 18. lungs 19. tissue 20. antibody.

1. do not connect; 2. 7; 3. 13.

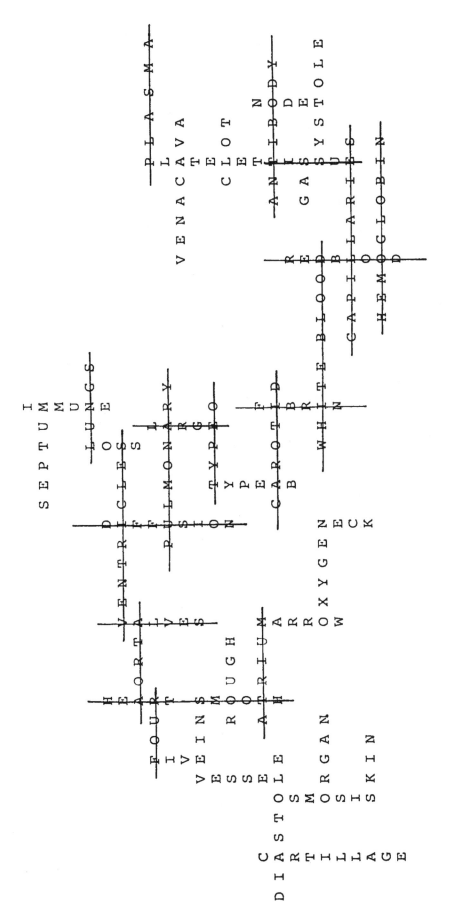

Health and Human Diseases

41. Twenty Broken Health Terms

adrenaline	bronchi	hemophilia	pituitary
amylase	endocrine	holistic	remission
arthritis	enzyme	interferon	symptom
benign	genetic	lymph	thymus
biopsy	glaucoma	nutrient	vaccine

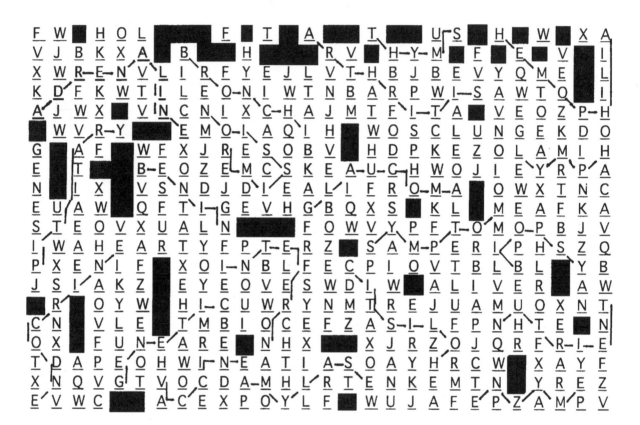

42. The ABC's of Infectious Diseases

Letter a: 1. amebic 2. animals 3. antibiotics 4. active 5. athlete's 6. anxiety

Letter b: 1. brain 2. bacteria 3. bubonic 4. blood 5. blood stream 6. body

Letter c: 1. cold 2. cough 3. contact 4. chicken 5. cilia 6. cells

disease, rash, burns, bruises, etc.

43. Word Within a Word

1. pill 2. rest 3. shot 4. cope 5. care 6. mend 7. fun 8. fresh 9. ease 10. peak 11. live 12. air 13. skin 14. fat 15. gene 16. mineral 17. milk 18. mind 19. body 20. well.

Items 18 and 19: A sound mind and healthy body is an excellent combination.

Items 13 and 19: The skin is the first line of defense for the body.

Item 15: Healthy genes help produce a strong body.

44. Five Letters

    1. health 2. acne 3. calorie 4. disease 5. diagnose 6. senile 7. retina 8. saliva 9. emotion 10. goiter 11. hormone 12. iris 13. medicine 14. obese 15. edema.

    Alphabetical Order: 1. acne 2. calorie 3. diagnose 4. disease 5. edema 6. emotion 7. goiter 8. health 9. hormone 10. iris 11. medicine 12. obese 13. retina 14. saliva 15. senile.

    A word describing how #5 and #7 are alike: swelling.

    A word describing how #10 and #13 are alike: eye.

45. Follow the Path

    1. virus 2. sprain 3. neuron 4. nicotine 5. epidermis 6. saliva 7. arteries 8. sweat 9. thyroid 10. dosage 11. emphysema 12. amnesia.

Ecology

46. Biotic Beings

    A. *Animals:* 1. trout 2. hawk 3. sparrow 4. eagle 5. bass 6. perch 7. goat 8. worm 9. snail 10. wolf 11. ape 12. buffalo 13. gopher 14. pig 15. mongoose. *Plants:* 1. pine 2. grass 3. fern 4. hay 5. alga.

    Possible responses for Part B: 1, 2, 3, and 4.

    1. Object A is an "F." F stands for fauna (animal life). All organisms in Object A are part of the fauna.

    2. Object B is a "P." P stands for plants. All organisms in Object B are plants.

    3. Object C is an "L." L stands for land. All organisms in Object C are land animals.

    4. Object D is an upside down "A." A stands for air. All organisms in Object D fly in the air.

    C. Birds
       INSECTS
       FOSSILS
       TREES
       CONIFERS
       COAL

47. Abiotic Adventure

    Possible Responses: A - air B - bed C - clay, crust, caliche D - dust, dirt E - emerald F - fire, flame G - glass H - hydrogen, helium I - ice J - jade K - kettle L - light M - magma, mud, mud-flow N - nitrogen, neon O - oxygen P - puck Q - quartz, quartzite R - rock S - soil T - table U - umbrella V - violin W - water X - xylophone Y - yarn Z - zinc.

    Bonus: bib, cot, and bit.

48. Ecosystem Wordsearch

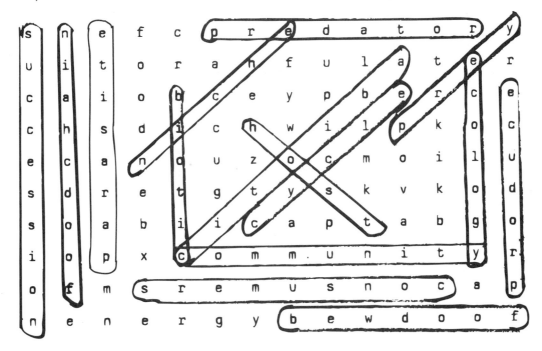

1. biotic 2. abiotic 3. community 4. ecology 5. niche 6. succession 7. parasite 8. producer 9. prey 10. food chain 11. host 12. cycle 13. food web 14. consumers 15. predator.

Mini-Puzzlers #1: bacteria #2: organism: bat; organism's habitat: cave.

49. Mixed Up Biomes

A and B lined out words: Tundra - cactus, palm; Coniferous Forests - zebra, bison; Deciduous Forests - platypus, cheetah; Tropical Rain Forest - maple, redwood; Grasslands - caribou, sequoia; Desert - alga, fern.

C. *Plants:* 1. cactus 2. palm 3. redwood 4. sequoia 5. alga 6. fern 7. maple *Animals:* 1. caribou 2. cheetah 3. platypus 4. bison 5. zebra.

D. 1. cheetah 2. zebra.

E. *Plants:* Largest - redwood; Smallest - lichen

   Animals: Largest - bison; Smallest - mouse

50. Water Biomes

A and B - *Fresh Water:* 1. alga 2. bluegill 3. carp 4. clam 5. crappie 6. frog 7. pike 8. salmon 9. snail 10. sturgeon.

C. 1. snail 2. clam.

D. *Salt Water:* 1. abalone 2. alga 3. clam 4. lobster 5. salmon 6. snail 7. squid 8. sturgeon 9. tuna 10. whale.

E. 1. lobster 2. clam 3. snail 4. abalone.

F. ESTUARY *Last Hint:* The *first* letters of the *first* words in Sentences 2, 3, 5, and 6 fill the empty spaces (from left to right) to form ESTUARY.

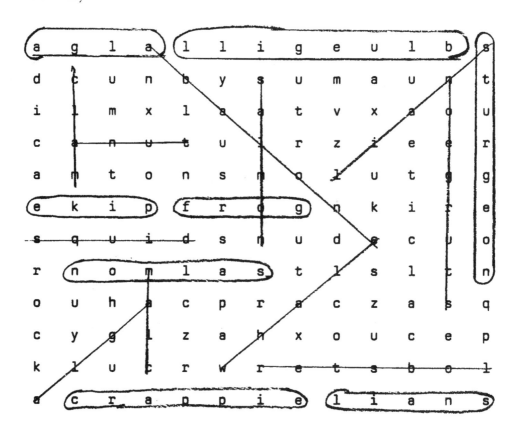

Section Two:
Physical Science
Energy

51. Energy Is Energy

1. two 2. al+ten+po+ti=potential 3. Energy on the move is *kinetic* energy. 4. high energy 5. low energy 6. a bundle of energy 7. Drop the Y and arrange the rest of the letters to spell GREEN 8. N "err" G

9.　　1　　　　　　　　　　　10. A buildup of ENERGY.
　　kinetic
　　　g
　　heat
　　t

52. Six Types

A. 1. mechanical (extra: ng) 2. heat (extra: i) 3. radiant (extra: n) 4. nuclear (extra: t) 5. chemical (extra: li) 6. sound (extra: gh). B. lightning. C. Three forms of energy.

53. Energy Is As Energy Does

A. Numbers 2, 4, 6, 8, 11, 14, and 15.

B. Numbers 1, 3, 7, 9, and 10.

C. The word is net (ki*net*ic); possible answers are fishing, playing tennis, playing volleyball, playing table tennis, playing basketball and playing badminton. D. The word is tent (po*tent*ial); possible answers are kettle of water, logs for fuel, lamp fuel, flashlight battery, jerky (dried meat), and so on.

54. Energy Crossword

Across: 1. electrical 3. ear 4. kinetic 6. light 8. potential 9. energy 11. atomic 14. convection 16. mechanical.

Down: 2. energy 5. ch*emical* 7. created 10. radiant 12. conduction 13. sound 15. calorie 17. law.

55. Mixed-Up Energy

1. Energy is the ability or capacity to do work. 2. The sun provides solar energy. 3. Fuels are burned to change chemical energy into heat energy. 4. Potential energy is also known as stored or resting energy. 5. Kinetic energy is energy of motion. 6. Splitting the atomic nucleus produces nuclear energy. 7. The merging of two or more atomic nuclei produces nuclear energy. 8. Energy cannot be created or destroyed but may be changed from one form to another. 9. Energy exists in different forms. 10. Radiant energy passes through space. 11. Large amounts of energy run machines to make consumer products. 12. Fossil fuels are a source of energy.

Sound

56. Sound Off

Across: 1. echoes 2. noise 4. music 5. volume 7. sol 10. harp 13. wave 14. snap.

Down: 1. ear 3. vps 5. vibration 6. eustachian 8. pitch 9. tone 11. vacuum 12. medium 13. whispers.

57. The Human Ear

1. inner ear 2. organ of Corti 3. outer ear 4. middle ear 5. hair cells 6. pinna 7. earwax 8. ossicles 9. malleus 10. incus 11. stapes 12. fluid 13. vestibule 14. cochlea 15. eardrum.

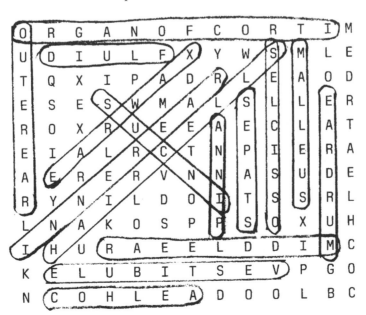

58. Matching Sounds

    1. 12   2. 8   3. 2   4. 10   5. 1   6. 9   7. 11   8. 7   9. 6   10. 4   11. 5   12. 3
    13. 19   14. 25   15. 24   16. 22   17. 23   18. 20   19. 21   20. 18   21. 15   22. 14
    23. 16   24. 17   25. 13.

59. The Speed of Sound

A.   1. travel 2. echo 3. water 4. slower 5. speed 6. time 7. measure 8. distance 9. solid 10. reflect 11. seconds 12. molecule 13. sound 14. bounce 15. liquid.

B.   Mystery Formula: 5=speed, 8=distance and 6=time.

C.   Mystery Problem: 1980 feet divided by 1.8 = 1100 feet per second.

D.   Possible Answers:

1.   *Sound* (13) may *reflect* (10) and return as an *echo* (2).

2.   *Sound* (13) may *travel* (1) through a *liquid* (15) or *solid* (9).

3.   The *speed* (15) of *sound* (13) may be determined by dividing *time* (6) into *distance* (8).

60. Very Sound Riddles and Problems

A.   1. a p*ear* 2. a rat - vib*rat*ions. Without "rat" the word vibrations would not exist. 3. a hunting dog - h*ound*. 4. One *tone*. 5. Because they know from experience that sound (and dust) travel through a vacuum. 6. You need to *see* a dog whistle.

B.
```
      s
s o u n d
    l
    i
    d
```

2.
```
      w a t e r
    _____
s o u n d   w a v e s
```

3.

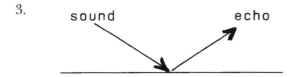

4.   Four - two *sounds,* one scream and one shout.

5.   P*ITCH*

6.   H*ear*t

Light

61. An "I" For An Eye

A.
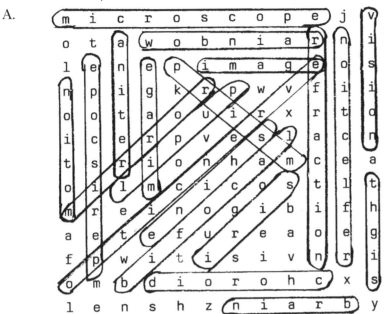

B. Terms: 1. bifocal 2. brain 3. choroid 4. image 5. iris 6. microscope 7. mirage 8. mirror 9. motion 10. optic nerve 11. periscope 12. prism 13. pupil 14. rainbow 15. reflection 16. refraction 17. retina 18. shine 19. sight 20. vision.

C. 1. choroid 2. iris 3. optic nerve 4. pupil 5. retina.

D. 1. reflection 2. refraction 3. rainbow. E. 1. The *retina* (17) receives the *image* (4) and connects to the *brain* (2) by the *optic nerve* (10). 2. A *microscope* (6) and a *periscope* (11) are optical instruments.

62. Letters in a Box

1. sun 2. light 3. straight lines 4. reflection 5. opaque 6. mirror 7. concave 8. refraction 9. convex 10. spectrum 11. color 12. optics.

63. Let There Be Light

1. bulb 2. eye 3. sun 4. glowworm 5. lightning 6. prism 7. fire 8. flare 9. candle 10. star 11. flashbulb 12. explode 13. headlight 14. spotlight 15. telescope 16. solar cell 17. reflection 18. microscope 19. fireplace 20. refraction 21. fireworks 22. spark 23. daylight 24. periscope.

64. Light Statements

1. travels 2. mirage 3. iris 4. reflect 5. separates 6. optics 7. refracted 8. color 9. frequency 10. retina 11. vision 12. particles 13. produce 14. combination 15. transparent 16. opaque 17. photons 18. straight 19. eight 20. translucent.

65. Missing Letters

    A. 1. a   2. y   3. t   4. e   5. h   6. n   7. a   8. t   9. o   10. e   11. i   12. r   13. g
    14. r   15. m   16. h   17. e   18. u   19. e   20. e   21. f   22. o   23. s   24. n
    25. h   26. s   27. s   28. a   29. n   30. i   31. l   32. g.

    B. 1. teh 2. yee 3. si 4. a 5. maunh 6. snees 7. ganor 8. orf 9. gihtl.

    C. Unscrambled Words: 1. the 2. eye 3. is 4. a 5. human 6. sense 7. organ 8. for 9. light.

    Mystery Statement: The eye is a human sense organ for light.

Electricity and Magnetism

66. Cross Terms

    1. attract 2. electricity 3. protons 4. electrons 5. neutron 6. battery 7. field 8. magnetism
    9. repulsion 10. poles 11. paper 12. compass 13. earth 14. current 15. plastic 16. lodestone.

67. Charged Up

    A. Puzzle

    B. 1. ampere 2. attract 3. battery 4. bulb 5. charge 6. current 7. electron 8. field 9. force
    10. iron 11. negative 12. neutral 13. neutron 14. north 15. pole 16. positive 17. proton
    18. repel 19. south 20. volt.

    C. Like charges repel each other.

68. Mix and Match

    A. 1. env*elop*e:pole 2. *leper*:repel 3. *wolf*hound:flow 4. *cray*on:arc 5. o*dor*:rod 6. *blub*ber:bulb
    7. *gulp*:plug 8. O*ttawa*:watt 9. *rab*bit:bar 10. P*lioce*ne:coil.

    B. 1. e 2. h 3. d 4. i 5. b 6. g 7. f 8. a 9. j 10. c.

69. All About Magnetism

    1. compass 2. magnetite 3. poles 4. repel 5. attract 6. iron 7. field 8. horseshoe 9. bar
    10. negative 11. positive 12. needle 13. force 14. electron 15. atom 16. nickel.

70. Eight Mini-Problems

    1. mAgnet. Ag is the chemical symbol for silver 2. Box B. Box B, the lightest box, weighs six
    pounds. Therefore, the *light* bulb most likely would be in this box. 3. You may use only one
    word, circuit, but you can use it twice. For example,

circuit		c	c	
	or	i	i	
circuit		r	r	
		c	c	and so on
		u	u	
		i	i	
		t	t	

    4. Separate the + into two –'s. Then write

    5. Electrolyte. The remaining four letters are "lyte."

    6. B and D represent "short" circuits.

7. Seven - six *amp*'s and one *ampere*.

8. Draw a line under or circle the *low* part of the word ki*low*att-hour.

Matter

71. Solid Phase

1. rubber 2. plastic 3. lumber 4. paper 5. automobile 6. chalkboard 7. chandelier 8. guitar 9. sponge 10. tambourine 11. trombone 12. stegosaur.

72. Liquid Phase

1. waterfall 2. precipitation 3. moisture 4. lemonade 5. breaker 6. tsunami 7. ocean 8. gasoline 9. steam 10. aqueous 11. petroleum 12. perspiration.

73. Gas Phase

1. carbon dioxide 2. oxygen 3. hydrogen 4. helium 5. chlorine 6. methane 7. propane 8. argon 9. carbon monoxide 10. neon 11. butane 12. ethane.

74. Mixed Matter

A. 1. tin 2. rain 3. rice, ice 4. rag 5. tile 6. ore 7. argon 8. air 9. iron 10. dime 11. nit 12. log 13. neon 14. mist, hem 15. prop, rope 16. bile, auto 17. ale 18. asp 19. oil 20. rink, ink.

B. W-*w*asp 2. Both metal, both solid 3. Iron and tin are metals produced from ores 4. a. brain b. grain c. train d. sprain

75. Puzzling Matter

Across: 6. properties 7. malleable 10. oxygen 11. matter 13. melting 15. space 17. special 19. density 22. substance 23. chemical 24. ductile 26. phase 27. plasma.

Down: 1. sublimate 2. water 3. solid 4. gas 5. weight 8. chemistry 9. volume 12. glass 14. mass 16. freezing 18. elasticity 20. physical 21. particle 25. change.

Atomic Structures

76. Boxed In

1. nucleus 2. electrons 3. neutral 4. neutrons 5. protons 6. number 7. symbol 8. ion 9. level 10. atom 11. mass 12. periodic 13. ion 14. symbol 15. protons 16. neutral.

77. Elements Everywhere

1. xenon 2. lead 3. Einsteinium 4. cadmium 5. cerium 6. zinc 7. antimony 8. astatine 9. neon 10. silver 11. selenium 12. carbon 13. oxygen 14. Lawrencium 15. lithium 16. nickel 17. curium 18. copper.

78. Say What?

1. particles for articles 2. single for pringle 3. smallest for tallest 4. blocks for stocks 5. nucleus for gluteus 6. neutral for normal 7. neutrons for newtons 8. charge for barge 9. travels for unravels 10. rapid for rabid 11. clouds for crowds 12. mass for pass 13. quarks for quartz 14. protons for croutons 15. electrons for rejectons 16. latin for satin 17. chemical for comical 18. symbol for thimble 19. silver for sliver 20. isotope for isopod.

79. Chemical Symbol Parade

1. As,P,Cl=ClAsP 2. Th,Pa=PaTh 3. Ce,Ra=RaCe 4. N,Co,Ra,O=RaCoON
5. Dy,B,O,N,O=NOBODy 6. La,Ce,N=LaNCe 7. O,C,B,Ra=COBRa
8. Ba,Rh,Rb,U=RhUBaRb 9. Er,O,Rh,Os,C,In=RhInOCErOs 10. Ar,N,Lu=LuNAr
11. N,Br,O,Co=BrONCo 12. Er,Po,K=PoKEr 13. B,Cr,I=CrIB 14. H,Ar,N,Al,W=NArWHAl
15. S,P,N,O,Er=PErSON 16. Ir,P,Ta=TaPIr 17. Ru,S,W,Al=WAlRuS 18. Ca,In,B=CaBIn
19. Na,Ti,Re=ReTiNa 20. Ti,C,Ac=CAcTi.

80. Where Are They?

1. R*hen*ium (75) 2. *anti*mony (51) and l*anth*anum (57) 3. asta*tine* (85) pla*tin*um (78) act-
*in*um (89) and protac*tini*um (91) 4. g*alli*um (31) 5. n*eon* (10) 6. g*old* (79) 7. ti*tani*um (22)
8. b*oron* (5) 9. th*alli*um (81) 10. m*agn*esium (12) 11. po*tassi*um (19) - possum 12. iridium
(77) and Einsteinium (99) 13. s*ulfu*r (16) 14. wren - La*wren*cium (103) 15. x*enon* (54) - one.

Chemistry

81. Chemistry Terms, Part 1

1. atom 2. gas 3. element 4. ion 5. liquid 6. compound 7. molecules 8. bond 9. matter
10. particle 11. solid 12. mixture 13. oxide 14. substance 15. crystal.

Mystery Item: Filtering

S	U	B	S	T	A	N	C	E	M
C	O	M	P	O	U	N	D	P	O
G	A	S	S	O	L	I	D	A	L
C	B	O	N	D	I	O	N	R	E
R	O	X	I	D	E	I	R	T	C
Y	T	A	T	O	M	L	E	I	U
S	G	M	A	T	T	E	R	C	L
T	I	L	I	Q	U	I	D	L	E
A	M	I	X	T	U	R	E	E	S
L	F	N	E	L	E	M	E	N	T

82. Chemistry Terms, Part 2

1. solvent 2. mole 3. toxic 4. base 5. reactant 6. solution 7. alloy 8. radical 9. diatomic
10. subscript 11. catalyst 12. solute 13. salt 14. acid 15. miscible.

Mystery Item: Vertical Columns

R	S	U	B	S	C	R	I	P	T
E	S	O	L	U	T	I	O	N	C
A	D	I	A	T	O	M	I	C	A
C	M	V	U	B	A	S	E	L	T
T	O	E	S	O	L	U	T	E	A
A	L	C	A	L	L	O	Y	R	L
N	E	R	A	D	I	C	A	L	Y
T	A	C	I	D	S	A	L	T	S
N	S	O	L	V	E	N	T	O	T
I	M	I	S	C	I	B	L	E	C
T	S	M	T	O	X	I	C	L	A

83. Twist and Turn

1. sugar, sand 2. iron, sulfur 3. gravel, sticks 4. rice, peas 5. lettuce, beets, carrots 6. copper, lead, iron 7. salt, pepper 8. apples, oranges 9. nickel, dimes 10. sugar, salt.

A Challenge: mix*"tures"*

84. Compounds

A. 1. Mn,O,O=MnO_2 (manganese dioxide) 2. Si,O,O=SiO_2 (silicon dioxide) 3. C,O,O=CO_2 (carbon dioxide) 4. Na,Cl=NaCl (sodium chloride) 5. C,H,H,H,H=CH_4 (methane) 6. C,C,C,H,H,H,H,H,H,H,H=C_3H_8 (propane) 7. Cu,S,O,O,O,O=$CuSO_4$ (copper sulfate) 8. Ca,C,O,O,O,=$CaCO_3$ (calcium carbonate) 9. H,H,O,O=H_2O_2 (hydrogen peroxide) 10. Fe,Fe,O,O,O=Fe_2O_3 (iron(III) oxide).

B. hydrogen peroxide (H_2O_2) 2. silicon dioxide (SiO_2) 3. carbon dioxide (CO_2).

C. Bo+G+Us = BoGUs or a *bogus* compound.

85. Chemistry Mini-Problems

1. Numbers 77, 8 and 7 on the Periodic Table of Elements are the atomic numbers for Iridium (Ir), Oxygen (O) and Nitrogen (N) respectively. Put the chemical symbols together and you have IrON or *iron.* 2. Chemical change. 3. Matter going through a phase. 4. Prisoner - con, animal - rat, star - sol (Spanish name for sun is sol) and charged particle - ion. 5. Use the letters O,Y,G,E and N from anywhere in the illustration. Then use the crossed HYDROGENs as an X to complete the word OXYGEN. 6. As part of the Sodium Family (Na). 7. Freeze it! 8. Add a *g* to the *ram* and you'll have a *gram* which is equal to 1/1000 kilogram.

Heat

86. All About Heat

1. heater 2. energy 3. calorie 4. kinetic 5. thermal 6. zero 7. radiation 8. particle 9. melts 10. conductor 11. temperature 12. convection 13. Fahrenheit 14. candle 15. insulator 16. friction.

87. Every Other Letter

   A. 1. copper 2. ore 3. nickel 4. dynamite 5. chromium 6. tin 7. silver.

   B. 1. radiator 2. atmosphere 3. dancing 4. infrared 5. thermal 6. exercise 7. sunshine.

   C. Au - gold. Gold metal conducts heat.

88. It's in the Term

   1. a. cur b. rent 2. a. dia b. tio 3. a. tempera b. era 4. a. comb b. bus c. bust 5. a. he b. mal 6. a. oil b. poi 7. a. en b. dot c. other d. do 8. a. up b. erup from right to left would be *pure*.

89. Seven-Letter Puzzle

   A. Puzzle.

```
                          m                    cold              morse
            s   o   d     o             c       a       sold    tenom
         w  m   m   i     l    steam    a      old       oe        n
        wh  i   a   a     e                    i               te       o
        a  it k  l    p   c             r      r      o   late    n
        t   e e  i        u    eject    o      e      l          i    o
        e      a r        l             o      exit   d   s      o   t
        r        r        e    energy   exit                     n
```

   B. 1. Morse 2. Monet 3. eject 4. Alamo 5. exit.

   C. Nuclear energy.

90. Middle Letter Message

   1. alert 2. relax 3. erect 4. racer 5. water 6. large 7. quiet 8. special 9. write 10. pretzel 11. rayon 12. fighter 13. trend 14. crave 15. motel 16. mulch 17. smile 18. bogus 19. bighorn 20. pitch.

   ELECTRICITY becomes useful when it is converted into HEAT and LIGHT.

Force and Motion

91. Keen Machines

   A. 1. lathe 2. shovel 3. axle 4. scissors 5. shoehorn 6. wheelbarrow 7. screw 8. wedge 9. gear 10. bicycle 11. tongs 12. nutcracker 13. tractor 14. broom 15. rake 16. crowbar 17. hammer 18. winch 19. incline 20. pulley 21. piston.

   B. Mystery Statement: These are about machines.

92. Two Missing Letters

   A. 1. st 2. mo 3. ne 4. ch 5. gr 6. we 7. un 8. ac 9. re 10. po 11. ve 12. de 13. fr 14. in 15. fo.

   B. *d* 1. gr (5) + in (14) = grin *c* 2. ch (4) + in (14) = chin *g* 3. po (10) + st (1) = post *j* 4. mo (2) + ve (11) = move *h* 5. po (10) + re (9) = pore *i* 6. st (1) + un (7) = stun *a* 7. mo (2) + re (9) = more *e* 8. mo (2) + st (1) = most *b* 9. ac (8) + ne (3) = acne *f* 10. ac (8) + re (9) = acre.

93. Pyramid Power

   1. force (4) 2. inertia (5) 3. mass (4) 4. motion (2) 5. speed (2) 6. Newton (9) 7. laws (9) 8. accelerate (1) 9. weight (8) 10. distance (6) 11. action (7) 12. time (7).

94. Vowel Trouble

   A. 1. inertia 2. accelerate 3. velocity 4. friction 5. reaction 6. gravity 7. impetus 8. mass 9. energy 10. decelerate 11. unbalanced 12. action 13. distance 14. weight 15. centrifugal 16. Newton 17. direction 18. balanced 19. speed 20. momentum.

B. 1. 4   2. 16   3. 8   4. 17   5. 6   6. 10   7. 18   8. 5

95. A Mix of Riddles and Problems

1. *Mass*achusetts 2. Mom Entum - momentum 3. w + eight or w + 8. Then break the 8 down into two o's. Now you have w + o + o or "woo." 4. FORCES in EQUILIBRIUM - EQ*FU OIL-RICBREIUSM*. 5. Loss or reduction of FRICTION. 6. The center of balance. 7. Th + Fe$_2$O$_3$. The formula Fe$_2$O$_3$ stands for rust. Therefore, Th + FE$_2$O$_3$ = Th + rust or *Thrust*. 8. FORE - *FORCE*. 9. Science *Friction* 10. Changing SPEED 11. Falling objects. 12. A measure of GRAVITY.

A Potpourri of Physical Science Puzzles

96. Partly There

A. 1. cry*stal* 2. vol*ume* 3. *sub*stance 4. *press*ure 5. *amp*litude 6. nuc*lear* 7. mole*cule* 8. con*dense* 9. inten*sity* 10. *comp*ound 11. en*erg*y 12. *car*bon 13. *elec*tron 14. la*ser* 15. mag*netic* 16. *dens*ity 17. kin*etic* 18. *mac*hine 19. *iso*tope 20. *the*rmal.

B. 1. e 6. c 10. g. 17. a 11. h 4. d 20. b 12. f.

97. Mystery Question Wordsearch

1. helium 2. watt 3. acid 4. ampere 5. neutron 6. light 7. matter 8. orbit 9. solute 10. litmus 11. proton 12. gravity 13. echo 14. fission 15. chlorine 16. electron 17. symbols 18. hydrogen 19. velocity 20. opaque.

Ten Terms in Puzzle: 1. helium 2. acid 3. light 4. orbit 5. gravity 6. echo 7. fission 8. electron 9. symbols 10. velocity.

Mystery Question Answer: theory

98. Broken Word Maze

Puzzle

Terms: 1. solid 2. matter 3. alloy 4. fulcrum 5. energy 6. trough 7. crest 8. celsius 9. decibel 10. work 11. power 12. cohesion 13. speed 14. friction 15. adhesion.

99. Group of Four

A. 1. heat 2. acid 3. salt 4. base 5. ions 6. neon 7. kilo 8. xray 9. watt 10. volt 11. amps 12. zinc 13. iron 14. mass 15. work 16. ores 17. kiln 18. atom 19. bond 20. slag.

B. 1. ores, iron, zinc, and slag 2. iron, zinc, and neon 3. volt, amp, and watt 4. acid and base 5. atom, bond, and ions.

100. Best Match

1. sodium 2. Neptunium 3. carbon 4. chlorine 5. pull 6. rest 7. liquid 8. kinetic 9. pulley 10. copper 11. wax 12. crest 13. harmony 14. outward 15. inward 16. bend 17. neutron 18. electrons 19. heat 20. mass/volume 21. charged 22. negative 23. positive 24. split 25. unlike 26. smallest 27. measure 28. rate 29. space 30. like.

Section Three:
Earth Science
Minerals

101. Treasures of the Lithosphere

1. galena 2. diamond 3. talc 4. halite 5. fluorite 6. gypsum 7. graphite 8. orthoclase 9. hematite 10. pyrite 11. ice.

Friendly Challenge: sulfur, quartz, feldspar, serpentine.

102. Finding 15 Minerals

1. corundum 2. cinna*bar* 3. he*ma*tite 4. apatite 5. g*rap*hite 6. serpen*tine* 7. a*gate* 8. quartz 9. j*asp*er 10. c*halce*do*ny* 11. flint 12. topaz 13. fluorite 14. galena 15. magnetite.

103. Gem Mountain

1. diamond 2. beryl or topaz 3. jade or opal 4. opal or jade 5. garnet or zircon 6. corundum 7. zircon or garnet 8. topaz or beryl 9. tourmaline.

A Bit of Research: 1. aquamarine 2. emerald 3. sapphire 4. ruby.

104. Mineral Maze

1. lead 2. fracture 3. yellow 4. Mohs 5. mica 6. emerald 7. quartz 8. calcite 9. hardness 10. garnet 11. diamond 12. refracts 13. cleave 14. luster 15. fluorite 16. talc 17. halite 18. magnetite 19. ice 20. quartz.

Shortest path from Entrance to Exit: lead, diamond, yellow, luster, emerald, fracture, garnet, cleave and magnetite.

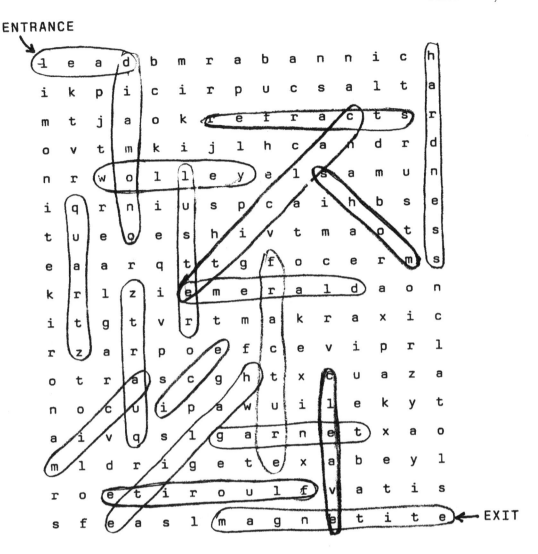

105. Where in the Word?

1. tin 2. tap 3. maid 4. sum 5. tame 6. tag 7. mite 8. copy 9. cram 10. tired 11. lag 12. nit 13. inn 14. cry 15. nina 16. spa 17. tour 18. rap 19. wolf, ram 20. sure 21. cup 22. lap 23. ox 24. alga 25. nay.

Rocks

106. Twelve Igneous Rocks

Answers may be in any order.

A. 1. diorite (1) 2. andesite (11) 3. scoria (10) 4. felsite (9) 5. obsidian (20) 6. granite (19) 7. tuff (17) 8. basalt (3) 9. gabbro (7) 10. syenite (22) 11. rhyolite (5) 12. pumice (21).

B. 145

C. 12.083333

D. 12

E. The answer *12* is the number of igneous rocks to identify in the activity.

107. Metamorphic Scatter

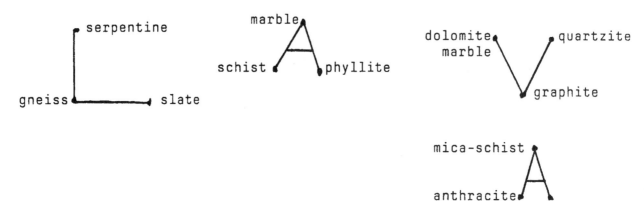

Mystery Question Answer: lava

108. Scrambled Sedimentary Wordsearch

1. breccia 2. chalk 3. conglomerate 4. gypsum 5. halite 6. limestone 7. marl 8. sandstone 9. shale 10. travertine.

Research It!

1. gypsum 2. rock salt 3. shale 4. marl 5. conglomerate.

109. Rock Talk

Sedimentary Rocks: layered, deposited by water, deposited by wind, ice deposits, shale, limestone, sandstone, conglomerate, salt and sand and gravel.

Igneous Rocks: fire origin, magma, batholith, laccolith, breccia, lava, tuff, granite, basalt, and pumice.

Metamorphic Rocks: heat and pressure, warped crust, folded crust, fine banding, foliation, marble, quartzite, schists, gneiss and slate.

110. Rock Riddles

1. A rock head 2. Remove the "oc" in rock. Put the *c* in front of the *O* and place the "co" combination before the rk, hence *cork*. 3. A dime - se*dime*ntary layer of earth. 4. Near the middle - m*ag*ma - Ag is the chemical symbol for silver. 5. The last half: ice; pum*ice*. 6. Shale under pressure produces slate. 7. Limestone under pressure produces marble. 8. None of the quartz and only one half of the sc*his*t, the "his" part. 9. Sandst*one*. Sandstone always finishes "Number *one*." 10. Because it has an inner "glo" - con*glo*merate. 11. Much of it consists of a yen - s*yen*ite. 12. It has two "c's" in its makeup. 13. One - c*rock*. 14. Because the girl's name might be Roxanne Pebbles. 15. Fold*ing*.

Weathering and Erosion

111. Weathering Challenge

A. Tornado, hail, tree roots, hurricane, water, rain, sleet, frost action, blizzard, sun, snow, wind and gravity.

B. Rain, snow, and hail. *Answer to question:* They are all related to water.

C. 1. shoulders - boulders 2. mouse - house 3. toads - roads 4. small - wall 5. pound - ground.

112. Chemical Weathering

    A. 1. water 2. substances, chemical 3. swell, break 4. dioxide, carbonic 5. limestone, marble 6. decomposition 7. clay, iron 8. chemical, mechanical 9. acid rain 10. plant decay.

    B. 1. dioxide 2. chemical 3. decomposition 4. iron 5. clay.

113. Weathered Objects

    Here are some possible answers:

    A. M - mountains E - environment C - cliffs H - hallways A - aircraft N - nets I - igloos C - crust A - abutments L - levees.

    　　C - cars H - houses E - environment M - minerals I - igneous rocks C - caves A - anchors L - limestone.

    B. Possible responses: ring, gate, wreath, tin, hat, tire, garage, and so on.

114. Erosion Wordsearch

    1. creep 2. talus 3. landslide 4. desert 5. mudflow 6. breaker 7. ravine 8. water 9. moraine 10. topsoil 11. erosion 12. roots 13. stack 14. waterfall 15. wind 16. promontory 17. gully 18. floods 19. subsoil 20. rivers 21. slump 22. glacier 23. dams 24. gravity 25. canyon 26. runoff 28. deposition.

115. Erosion Explosion

    Erosion game. No answer key necessary.

Earth Features

116. Earth Vibrations

    A. 1. fault 2. tremor 3. seismology 4. focus 5. epicenter 6. primary 7. secondary 8. Richter 9. tsunami.

    B. Answers will vary for 1, 2, and 3.

    C. 1. tsunami 2. Richter 3. focus 4. secondary 5. primary.

117. The Big Boom

    Chart　　Areas: 1. gases, cinders 2. gases 3. crater 4. vent, neck 5. lava: basalt, pumice 6. cone, side 7. dike, extreme heat and pressure 8. dike, extreme heat and pressure 9. laccolith, extreme heat and pressure 10. magma, extreme heat and pressure 11. sill, extreme heat and pressure 12. batholith, extreme heat and pressure.

118. Glacier Mixup

    1. An ice age is a period of very cold temperatures.
    2. Glaciers thrive during ice ages.
    3. The last ice age ended about 11,000 years ago.
    4. Glaciers exist today in very cold climates.
    5. The ice in many glaciers is over 1,000 feet thick.
    6. The base of the ice is under great pressure.

7. Glaciers move at a slow pace.
8. Gravity and the weight of the ice cause glaciers to move.
9. Valley glaciers form in mountains and move slowly downhill through valleys.
10. Continental glaciers are great sheets of ice covering a large area.
11. Glaciers carve out valley floors.
12. Glaciers are agents of erosion.
13. Glaciers carry rock debris with tons of ice.
14. Glaciers deposit silt, sand, and large fragments known as till.
15. A moraine is a glacial deposit of till.
16. End moraines form at the edge of the ice sheet.
17. Drift refers to all the materials deposited by a glacier and its meltwaters.

119. Earth Features By Design

Here are some possible designs.

1. Volcano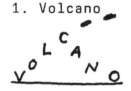

2. Fault

3. Mountain

4. Anticline

5. Syncline

6. Stalactite

7. Stalagmite

8. Ravine

9. Sediments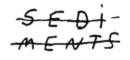

10. Iceberg

11. Plateau

12. Submarine Canyon

120. Missing Features

A. b - beach c - cave f - fault g - glacier i - island l - levee m - mantle o - ocean p - plate q - quartz r - rocks s - sediment t - trench u - uplift v - volcano w - wind.

B. 1. Quartz, a mineral, helps make up certain rocks.

2. Granite rock is partly made of quartz; rock and quartz exist in the Earth's crust, and so on.

C. 1. Quartz is a mineral; a rock is made from several different minerals.

2. Quartz has a hardness of 7; a rock may be hard or soft.

D. Both are agents of erosion.

Fossils

121. Fossil Candidates

A. 1. snail 2. bean 3. leaf 4. toad 5. housefly 6. iguana 7. tortoise 8. fruit 9. goat 10. trout.

B. 1. trout 2. goat 3. tortoise 4. snail 5. toad 6. iguana.

C. The trout has a bony skeleton. Therefore, it has more hard parts than an apple.

D. Possible responses: goat, oat, log, eel, gnat, plant, pony, alga, goon, loon, and so on.

122. Organisms Found As Fossils

Across: 2. coral 3. starfish 4. trilobite 5. fish 6. brachiopod 7. marsupial 8. gastropod 9. sponge 10. cycads 11. ammonites 12. reptiles.

Down: 1. fossiliferous sandstone.

123. 10 Mysterious Dinosaurs

1. tyrann 2. docus 3. losaurus 4. tri 5. stego 6. odon 7. al 8. rodon 9. iguan 10. ichthy.

Mystery Question Answer: sand (*DINOSAUR* - D, N, S, and A = SAND).

124. Bits and Pieces

Starfish: 1, 2, 4, 8, and 12; *Crinoid:* 3, 6, 7, and 11; *Brachiopod:* 5 and 9; *Ammonite:* 10, 13, and 14.

Mystery question possible answers: volcanism, faulting, glaciation, uplifting, overturning, and so on.

125. Fossil Riddles

1. trilobites 2. scattered *fossils* 3. a moth - mam*moth* 4. Because "mum's" the word - *mummi*-fy 5. *petri*fied 6. a petri*fried* tree 7. In the state of preservation 8. Fossil Records 9. fossil*ize* - "i's" 10. The "ail" part - sn*ail*.

126. Clouds About

A. sky, winds, condensation, cumulus, moisture, stratus, nimbus, precipitation, thunderstorms, sleet.

B. i u s r c r = cirrus

C. c s b u u u o n i m m l = cumulonimbus

D. Possible Answers: 1. Both are cloud types. 2. Sleet is frozen moisture. 3. Strong winds accompany thunderstorms. 4. Nimbus clouds carry precipitation.

E. Moisture, condenses, heavy, droplets fall

Moisture condenses; heavy droplets fall.

127. Tornado Power

1. water spouts 2. Kansas 3. tornado belt 4. funnel 5. spinning 6. late 7. everything 8. ground 9. earth 10. humid 11. path 12. miles per hour 13. minutes 14. whirling.

128. Twenty Weather Terms

A. 1. weather 2. condensation 3. warm front 4. humidity 5. wind 6. cirrus 7. climate 8. anemometer 9. breezes 10. psychrometer 11. stratus 12. cumulus 13. cloud seeding 14. precipitation 15. front 16. barometer 17. thermometer 18. thunder 19. sleet 20. tornado.

B. 1. Torricelli 2. thunderstorm

129. Weather Word Scramble

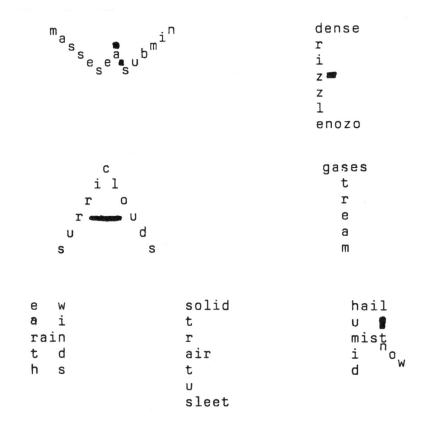

A. 1. nimbus 2. dense 3. gases 4. cirrus 5. stream 6. ice 7. mist 8. ozone 9. clouds 10. sleet 11. drizzle 12. air 13. sea 14. Earth 15. winds 16. humid 17. stratus 18. hail 19. masses 20. rain 21. solid.

B. STORM

130. Figure It Out

    1. cyclones - cy*clones*

    2. climates - cli*mates*

    3. *Weather* - water (5 out of 7 letters = 71+ percent.)

    4. Four - three *winds* and one *breeze*

    5. Crosswinds

    6. Calm *before* the storm

    7. Three rainbows

    8. z's - *zz*

    9. Saturation point

    10. Unsettled weather

    11. A mixture of stratus and cumulus

    12. A jet stream

Oceanography

131. Sea Life

    A. 1. barnacle 2. cod 3. coral 4. crab 5. eel 6. lobster 7. mollusk 8. perch 9. ray 10. scallop.

    B. 1. algae 2. anchovy 3. anemone 4. clam 5. diatom 6. oyster 7. plankton 8. porpoise 9. snail 10. tuna.

    C. Eel, cod and perch.

    D. Algae, snail, anchovy, tuna, oyster and clam.

    E. *Part A:* coral, barnacle, crab, lobster, mollusk and scallop. *Part B:* clam, diatom, and snail.

132. Hidden Treasure

    Terms: 1. guyot 2. tsunami 3. tide 4. trench 5. atoll 6. algae 7. trough 8. crest 9. ooze 10. shelf 11. current 12. basin 13. reef 14. island.

    Mystery Question Answer: sonar

133. Undersea Mystery

    1. 6e 2. 1m 3. 1b 4. 4d 5. 1n 6. 7h 7. 1l 8. 1a 9. 2c 10. 4j 11. 7f 12. 2k 13. 6i 14. 8g.

    Profile:

    Mystery Question Answer: seamount

134. The Big Eight

    1. six 2. lost 3. strong undertow 4. atom (di*atom*) 5. coral 6. NA (na) cl. NaCl is sodium chloride or salt. 7. seashore 8. two *boats* crossing *an ocean.*

135. The Ocean Floor

A.
```
s q s e g d i r n a o c o d i m
t d d n o o m p l a m l w s f e
a n v a l l e y s f v s t g y n
r t k j o b t k m a t r i z k s
s i c p i l u c r i u z e a e x
n n l o p p r h e p t s o g i g
i e m a z u y l m k r i n n t u
a n f q s a p a o x r a b w e y
t t a l g e e n e k c e a p v p
h a b y s s a l p l a i n i e t
u l v u p l u t o p h q m a r g
o s f s u n e v a t r k s g o a
m b m t e r o c k s s l n r v o
s e d i m e n t s a d c s a w j
h l e j d h t r a e h f l c b i
v f k m t s t h e l e n s a m a
c p o l s l a t n e n i t n o c
```

B. Plain; valley, trench, or canyon; plain, valley; mountain, seamount, volcano.

C. Salt water - salt H_2O

Nonrenewable Energy Sources

136. Coal Game

No answers required.

137. Mini-Problems

1. _pressure_ 2. Lignite (l*ignite*). 3. If you remove C, COAL would
   coal

disappear. *C* is the chemical symbol for carbon and coal is carbon. 4. S*oil*. 5. Four times: three *gas* and one *petroleum*. 6. An excellent example of nonrene*wable*. 7. h + ant + rac + e + it = hantraceit or *anthracite*. 8. Used up faster than it can be replaced by nature.

138. Disappearing Materials

A.

s	d	l	o	g	c	e	s
a	i	t	o	r	o	g	u
n	o	l	s	a	p	r	l
d	d	a	v	v	p	a	f
s	n	r	n	e	e	v	u
d	e	o	■	l	r	e	r
i	r	o	n	g	o	l	d
i	c	o	p	p	e	r	r

B. Uranium

C. Bonus Question Answer: restore

139. Going, Going…

1. sand 2. propane 3. galena 4. iron 5. methane 6. nickel 7. peat 8. gravel 9. bauxite 10. gasoline 11. copper 12. bituminous 13. uranium 14. hematite 15. mercury 16. anthracite 17. lignite 18. coal 19. oil 20. silver.

140. Nine Boxes

1. hydrocarbon 2. fossil fuel 3. coal 4. anthracite 5. bituminous 6. swamps 7. refinery 8. kerosene 9. lignite.

Mystery Question Answer: petroleum

Renewable Energy Sources

141. Fun With the Sun

A. 1. fusion 2. convection 3. flare 4. yellow 5. light 6. solar 7. corona 8. helium 9. prominence 10. hydrogen 11. energy 12. fission 13. star 14. chromosphere or photosphere 15. radiation 16. sunshine 17. gas 18. sunspot 19. heat 20. chromosphere or photosphere.

B. 1. yellow 2. sunshine 3. star 4. helium 5. hydrogen 6. energy

C. Answers will vary. Example: The sun's a *star* that produces *yellow sunshine*.

D. Answers will vary. Example: *Hydrogen* changes into *helium* and produces *energy*.

142. Water Words

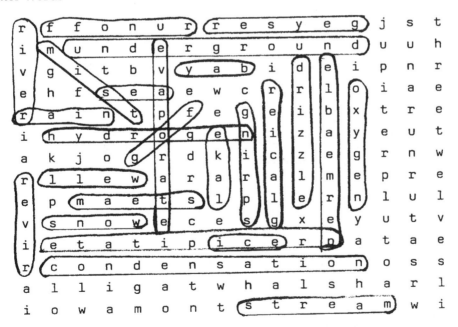

1. bay (L) 2. condensation (L) 3. drizzle (L) 4. evaporate (G) 5. fog (L) 6. geyser (L) 7. glacier (S) 8. hydrogen (G) 9. ice (S) 10. lake (L) 11. mist (L) 12. oxygen (G) 13. permeable (L) 14. precipitate (L,S) 15. rain (L) 16. river (L) 17. runoff (L) 18. sea (L) 19. snow (S) 20. spring (L) 21. steam (L) 22. stream (L) 23. underground (L) 24. well (L).

143. Five Renewable Energy Sources

    1. satellite 2. Uranus 3. neutron 4. weather 5. igneous 6. nebula 7. density 8. wind 9. anthracite 10. tsunami 11. erosion 12. rocks 13. fossil 14. oceanography 15. refraction 16. era 17. Saturn 18. tornado 19. solar 20. atom 21. ion 22. revolution.

144. Renewable Energy Mini-Problems

    1. solar 2. cross wind 3. H+H+O = H_2O 4. solar cells 5. 4 (four) + FeO (iron oxide or rust) = forest 6. steam underground 7. water (H_2O) table 8. a mixture of water, sun, and wind 9. "George is a human solar collector" 10. a *renewable energy source* is one that never runs out because it is constantly replaced.

145. Can You Find Them?

    A. breeze, motion, air, heat, and belt.

    B. current, flow, solid, liquid, and wet.

    C. gas, light, energy, eclipse, and life.

    D. leaves, plants, wood, trees, and tropical.

Astronomy

146. Plenty of Planets

    Left to Right: *Part One:* SATURN (RE), MARS (RN), PLUTO (EA), JUPITER (SX), EARTH (RT), NEPTUNE (TR), MERCURY (EI), VENUS (AT), URANUS (LA). *Part Two:* 1. Mercury 2. Venus 3. Earth 4. Mars 5. Jupiter 6. Saturn 7. Uranus 8. Neptune 9. Pluto. *Part Three:* AN EXTRATERRESTRIAL.

147. Mr. Sol

    1. so*lo*tude 2. de*sol*ate 3. *sol*ace 4. re*sol*ve 5. *sol*emn 6. ab*sol*ve 7. *sol*vent 8. dis*sol*ve 9. *sol*d 10. i*sol*ate 11. *sol*ution 12. *sol*ar 13. *sol*itaire 14. *sol*icit 15. *sol*o 16. con*sol*idate 17. con*sol*e 18. in*sol*ent 19. ab*sol*ute 20. *sol*stice 21. *sol*id 22. *sol*e 23. ga*sol*ine 24. *sol*ution 25. *sol*dier 26. obso*le*te.

148. The Moon

    1. albedo 2. crater 3. lunar 4. Copernicus 5. satellite 6. crescent 7. eclipse 8. phases 9. Tycho 10. volcanoes 11. depression 12. meteorite 13. maria 14. moonquakes 15. orbit 16. waxing 17. waning.

149. Planetary Puzzle

    1. atmosphere 2. clouds 3. craters 4. Earth 5. ellipse 6. gas 7. inner 8. Jupiter 9. light 10. Mars 11. mass 12. Mercury 13. moons 14. motion 15. Neptune 16. orbit 17. outer 18. path 19. phase 20. plains 21. Pluto 22. probe 23. rings 24. satellite 25. Saturn 26. sky 27. sun 28. telescope 29. Uranus 30. Venus.

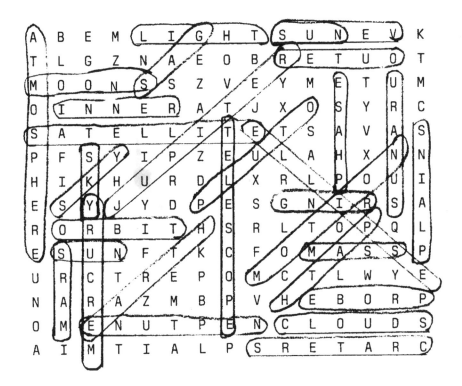

150. Space Bits

1. So there will be an *extra* terrestrial. 2. Satellite: MOON; Planet: MARS; A self-luminous gaseous celestial body: STAR. 3. A cavity-i.e., a *pit* - Ju*pit*er. 4. A rocky crust. 5. The Earth's twin 6. Asteroid 7. A meteorite crater 8. Moon erosion 9. From new moon to full moon. During this time the moon is waxing. 10. s,t,a,r = star.